The POWER of

TENACITY

—

The COURAGE of

LEADERSHIP

—

The STRENGTH of

CHARACTER

The POWER of

TENACITY

—

The COURAGE of

LEADERSHIP

—

The STRENGTH of

CHARACTER

by Peter Legge

with Tashon Ziara

Eaglet Publishing

Eaglet Publishing
Peter Legge Management Co. Ltd.
230, 4321 Still Creek Drive
Burnaby, British Columbia, V5C 6S7, Canada
Tel. (604) 299-7311 Fax (604) 299-9188

Library and Archives Canada Cataloguing in Publication

Legge, Peter, 1942-, author
     The 3 things you'll need to make your mark in life : the power of tenacity, the courage of leadership, the strength of character / by Dr. Peter Legge, OBC.

ISBN 978-0-9878194-4-4 (hardback)

     1. Determination (Personality trait). 2. Leadership. 3. Courage. 4. Success. I. Title. II. Title: Three things you will need to make your mark in life.

BF698.35.D48L44 2016   155.2'32   C2016-904993-0

Jacket design by Rick Thibert; cover image by Ron Sangha; electronic imaging by Mandy Lau; typeset by Ina Bowerbank; edited by Matt Currie
Printed and bound in Canada by Friesens

Dedication

To my wife Kay,

Who for almost fifty years has been my
greatest secret to a successful life.

You have loved me through good times and bad.

I never thought I could be loved
so unconditionally by one person.

You have always demonstrated tenacity,
leadership and character.

I love you,
Peter

TABLE OF CONTENTS

Part 3: The Strength Of Character

OTHER BOOKS BY THE AUTHOR

How to Soar With the Eagles
You Can If You Believe You Can
It Begins With a Dream
If Only I'd Said That
If Only I'd Said That: Volume II
If Only I'd Said That: Volume III
If Only I'd Said That: Volume IV
If Only I'd Said That: Volume V
If Only I'd Said That: Volume VI
Who Dares Wins
The Runway of Life
Make Your Life a Masterpiece
The Power of Tact
The Power to Soar Higher
The Power of a Dream
365 Days of Insights
Lunch With Joe
My Favourite Quotations

BOOKLETS

97 Tips on How to Do Business in Tough Times
97 Tips on Customer Service
97 Tips on How to Jumpstart Your Career

CD

The Runway of Life

FOREWORD

A LIFE OF STANDING OVATIONS

My earliest memories of Peter Legge are those of a chipper, likeable young man who I hired for the sales department of CKNW Radio in New Westminster, B.C. But his first ambition was to make people smile, laugh and feel good. So, he became a standup comedian. As the years wore on, Peter's time in front of a microphone onstage grew and grew. I've watched him with admiration. But soon, instead of jokes, his talks began focusing on more meaningful, inspiring messages. He was determined to become the most sought-after motivational speaker in the province, and he did. Recognitions and awards followed, including being named to the Speaker's Hall of Fame.

A Peter Legge talk always ends with a standing ovation. But the Peter Legge I knew and befriended back in 1962 is more than a motivational speaker. His small magazine company became one to be reckoned with when he purchased *BC Business* from Jimmy Pattison. He promised Jimmy he would develop the magazine into the best in the west. He has. Peter's print publications have made Canada Wide Media the most prolific in our province.

Those who read Peter's books or hear him speak know he

identifies me as one of his mentors. I suspect no one, with the possibility of the amazing Joe Segal, has lunched more with Peter to share thoughts and ideas. We're more than mentors. We're friends who admire and applaud his well-deserved success, and proudly give him a standing ovation.

Mel Cooper, CM, OBC, LL.D. (HON)
Chair, TELUS Victoria Community Board
Proud Mentor of Peter Legge

INTRODUCTION

Michelangelo once said, "And yes, I am still learning." Charlie "Tremendous" Jones, who was a member of the prestigious Speakers Roundtable group, said: "You will be the same person you are today in 20 years, except for the people you meet, the places you and go and the books you read."

The working title of my 20th book was: *This Is What I Know for Sure*. As a matter of fact, my speech on that same subject has become one of my most requested of all time.

Having celebrated 42 years in business, Canada Wide Media has grown from one title – *TV Week* magazine – to over 25 titles, as well as newsletters, websites and a host of highly successful annual events: from the *BCBusiness* 30 Under 30 (which honours those young CEOs, entrepreneurs and philanthropists who are excelling professionally and innovating in their industries) to the Craft Beer Festival, to the series of highly sought-after workshops we present each year, to the celebrated *BCBusiness* Top 100 event, which we have staged for almost 30 years.

The Top 100 event has grown from humble beginnings to become the most successful and most-attended networking luncheon/speaker presentation in the city. More than 1,000 people pack the Fairmont Hotel Vancouver each June to network, be seen and listen to some of B.C.'s – and indeed,

North America's – top business leaders. Here they learn and grow, take notes, look for some sage advice they can put to work in their own lives and rub elbows with the province's movers and shakers.

This highly anticipated event has presented speakers including the likes of Frank Abagnale (whose remarkable life story was dramatized in Steven Spielberg's *Catch Me If You Can*); billionaire entrepreneur Jimmy Pattison; my mentor of 50 years, the inimitable Joe Segal; Frank Giustra from Fiore Financial Corp; owner and operator of the Vancouver Canucks, Francesco Aquilini; and Richard Jaffray, president and founder of Cactus Club Café, to name just a few.

Here, you can meet a person, get an idea or even just a business card that you can follow up on; you can become inspired and motivated by the speaker; you can learn something to help your business grow or turn one of your ideas into action or improve your strategies. Almost anything is possible.

Audience members from the Top 100, as well as those who have attended other *BCBusiness* events call me regularly for advice on business or getting into the speaking profession. They ask: How have I run my business successfully for over 40 years? How do I weather the ups and downs of my industry? What is the secret to being an entrepreneur? How do I become an in-demand public speaker? The questions are endless and I am very flattered.

If you scan the Internet, everyone's got tips on how to be a success. So why aren't we all super successful?

The short answer is, because tips aren't enough. I have men and women approach me every day with big dreams. They dream of owning their own company; of delivering a TED Talk and influencing the world with their ideas; of inventing something that will solve a pressing global issue; or launching the next big social networking platform. These are worthy and admirable goals and I believe the people who share their dreams with me are absolutely sincere in their quest, but the truth is, the number of people who actually act on their dreams and make them happen is a very small number indeed.

But it doesn't have to be that way. There's not a finite amount of success to go around. I believe the majority of us have the capacity to succeed if we really want to, and if you're interested, I'd like to share with you what I've learned over the past 70-plus years about what it takes to make your mark on the world. Spoiler alert: it's not rocket science and you don't have to be the

> **"Nothing great in the world has ever been accomplished without passion."**
> — *GEORG WILHELM FRIEDRICH HEGEL*

smartest, the fastest or the first to be a success, but you do have to make a commitment and you do have to work at it. So why don't we get started!

People often wonder, what is the purpose of life? A better question: What is the purpose of *your* life?

PART 1

THE POWER
OF TENACITY

The quality of being determined to do or achieve something;
a firmness of purpose, staying power and endurance.

Tavistock Hall Preparatory School for Boys

*This photo is a framed piece of artwork given to me by the
school's headmaster, J.R. Ward, when I returned to celebrate the
50th anniversary of the school. Artist: Juliet Murray*

CHAPTER 1

A CALL TO ACTION

"To strive, to seek, to find, and not yield."
–Alfred Lord Tennyson

Winnifred Ivy Legge gave birth to her only child, a boy, at 7:02 a.m. on January 14, 1942. It was a typical English winter day, chilly and damp. That boy was me, Peter Bernard Legge.

The residential district where I was born was a small suburb called Ealing, just a few miles from central London. My parents had a small "flat" (what you might know as an apartment), in Greenford, Middlesex, just up the street from Ealing. We were on the second floor. Some 75 years later, that same apartment complex, called Brookfield Court, on Oldfield

Lane is still standing and apparently fully rented.

The Second World War started in 1939 and a ceasefire didn't come until six years later, in 1945. I really don't know how my parents worked and handled day-to-day life with a young son smack in the middle of a world war, particularly with the blitz of massive bombings going on in London and surrounding districts, but by all accounts Greenford was spared.

It must have been scary times, but is it possible that my parents' "tenacity" to live and build a home for a small family in the midst of such chaos might have rubbed off on me, even at that young age?

My father's family lived in Cadoxton, South Wales, seven short miles from the capital, Cardiff. He was one of nine siblings and lived on 10 Courtenay Road. Likely fearing for my safety, he asked his two sisters, Auntie Bette and Auntie Bun, to look after me for a while, as the war was raging and God only knew how long the blitz would go on for.

We certainly weren't rich and I still have no idea how my parents managed to afford a boarding school for me, but five days before my fifth birthday, I was shipped off to the Tavistock Hall Preparatory

> "It takes hunger, tenacity and commitment to see a dream through until it becomes a reality."
> — *JOHN C. MAXWELL*

School for Boys. I know now that my parents sent me there because they wanted to give me opportunities, but I'll tell you: with the uniforms and the strict discipline, it was tough for a young boy; you had to find ways to survive and fight to believe you were worthwhile.

The train ride from Heathfield to Victoria Station took 90 minutes, and that first year, I lived in fear that my parents might not be there to pick me up. There was no way to be in touch ahead of time.

At school, you only got the cane from the headmaster, J.R. Ward. Most of the time, it was two whacks on the rear end or occasionally four. If you really misbehaved, you were sent to his office for "six of the best."

At Tavistock I learned to take care of myself and to never give in to negative thoughts – and without realizing it I developed tenacity, which the Oxford dictionary describes as "the quality of not giving up easily, of holding on stubbornly."

That was in 1947, just a few months after the war ended. But before that happened, there was a tremendous party on my grandmother's street in Greenford to celebrate the return of peace, with loads of food, ice cream, sing-alongs and fires in the middle of the street. The mood was one of excitement, and anticipation of better times to come.

Thinking about that time now and imagining what it might have been like for my parents, I am humbled and awed by their tenacity, not only to marshal the resources to send me to a good school, but also, seven years later, to leave England altogether in the hopes of forging a better life in Canada.

CHAPTER 2

WHAT IS TENACITY?

When I asked Joe Segal what one characteristic is a sure-fire indicator that someone will turn out to be a successful person, he was quick to answer. "Tenacity!" he exclaimed, "the ability to pick yourself up, regroup and keep going when you encounter obstacles in your life."

According to Joe, failure is a fact of life and also a great learning opportunity. "The secret to success, the thing that many people never figure out," Joe told me, "is that we all fail many times before we succeed. I've always believed experience is the best teacher. I say, 'Show me a person who is a failure and I will show you someone who gave up while success still lay before them. Then show me a person who is a success and I will show you someone with many failures behind them.' Failure is an event, not a person."

Joe concluded that while having a special talent or ability is no doubt a great advantage, unless it is developed and applied it is no guarantee of success. Likewise, acquiring specialized knowledge or training can also contribute to your success; however, it is only valuable to the extent that you are prepared to apply it.

In the end, some of the most successful people in the world, including Joe himself – those who have excelled beyond what most of us could even imagine – are not the most talented or even the most educated. They are the individuals who are able to stand committed to one goal or purpose, come hell or high water.

I believe we first make our habits and then our habits make us.

Ivan Seidenberg tells a story about how hard work paid off early in his career. "My first boss was the building superintendent and I was a janitor. For almost a year, he watched me sweep floors and wash walls before he mentioned to me that I could get tuition for college if I got a job with the phone company. When I asked him why he'd waited so long to tell me this, he said, 'I wanted to see if you were worth it.' "

Seidenberg went on to have a 40-year career in the telecommunications industry, highlighted by his time as the chairman and CEO of global communications company Verizon.

Obstinance, determination, perseverance – call it what you like, these are the traits that characterize tenacity. Tenacity alone does not guarantee success. Many times the tenacious lose, but there is something to be gained by not giving up, and the fact remains: if you quit you'll never win. Here's a case in point. As a young man, Sylvester Stallone desperately wanted to break into acting. He was rejected repeatedly and told he would never be an actor because it was difficult to understand him when he spoke. Instead of giving up, Stallone wrote *Rocky*, but again, he faced rejection. Eventually, a producer agreed to buy the rights to *Rocky* for $256,000 as long as Stallone was not the star. That money could have gone a long way for the young actor, but it would not have fulfilled his dream. Instead, he agreed to $75,000 and 10 per cent of the net profits so he could be the star. Through his tenacity, Stallone attained exactly what he set out to.

There are many things you have to do to succeed . . . but none of that is going to happen by itself. You have to do the work and whether you want to call it willpower, persistence or determination, it is the key to success.

Do you think Nelson Mandela knew when he first chose to raise his voice against apartheid in South Africa that he would spend more than 27 years of his life in a prison cell?

Amazingly, when he was released, Mandela was neither bitter nor discouraged. With his optimism, hope and a willingness to forgive his captors and forge a new start, Nelson Mandela set an example for all of his countrymen and the entire world. He went on to become the first post-apartheid president of his country, to begin the process of reconciliation and healing between blacks and whites, and to realize his dream of a democratic South Africa. Who is to say what the world would look like today if Mandela had not had the tenacity to persevere?

Here is one of Mandela's most inspiring quotes; not surprisingly, it happens to be about tenacity: "Do not judge me by my successes, judge me by how many times I fell down and got back up again."

> **"Let me tell you the secret that has led me to my goal. My strength lies solely in my tenacity."**
> *— LOUIS PASTEUR*

CHAPTER 3

THE STRANGEST SECRET

If you think about nothing, the worst thing possible will happen: *nothing*. If you've read any of my books or been to a speaking event, you likely know my mantra: "We become what we think about most of the time." I speak of it often and I give credit to the aforementioned Earl Nightingale, who inspired me so many years ago and continues to do so to this day.

Nightingale, who was born in 1921 and died in 1989, was considered to be the dean of personal development for speakers, and he came to Vancouver a number of years ago as part of an all-day sales rally that I attended at the Pacific Coliseum. The emcee was Joe Kapp, former CFL quarterback for the BC Lions. In those days, all-day sales rallies were very common in North America. In excess of 12,000 people attended this one, including my entire sales department at Canada Wide Media – and we were not disappointed.

I had heard Nightingale's marvelous voice many times on the radio and his million-dollar message: "The Strangest Secret" as well as "We become what we think about." These two phrases have memorialized one of the greatest thinkers of our time and have literally changed my own thinking because it is so true: if we're really honest with ourselves, we are becoming or have become what our thoughts are.

Nightingale's premise was that of 100 people who start their careers at age 25 with the intent of being successful entrepreneurs or prosperous business leaders, only five per cent achieve their goals by the age of 65. In his book *The Strangest Secret*, he explored where the remaining 95 per cent went astray. According to Nightingale, success results from the pursuit of a worthy ideal.

Nightingale offers a simple yet powerful exercise to help us turn our thinking towards what it is we want to achieve.

First, write on a card what it is you want more than anything else. Perhaps you'd like to double your income or build a profitable business. It may be a new home. It may be a promotion at your job. It may be a particular career or role in life. It could be a better relationship with your spouse or someone else in your family.

Write down on your card specifically what it is you want.

Make sure it's a single goal and clearly defined. You don't need to show it to anyone else, just carry it with you so that you can look at it several times a day. Think about it in a relaxed, positive way each morning when you get up (it will give you something positive to focus on and a reason for getting out of bed). Look at it every chance you get during the day and also just before you go to bed at night. As you look at it, remember that you become what you think about, and since you're thinking about your goal, your mind will also begin to look for ways to help you achieve it.

Keep in mind, achieving you goal doesn't stop there. You have to be willing to take *action*. If you're not, you're not really thinking – you're simply daydreaming. So commit on a daily basis to pursue your goal with all the energy, enthusiasm and dedication that you can possibly muster.

CHAPTER 4

MAKE YOURSELF POSITIVELY UNCOMFORTABLE

If you've ever been to the top of a mountain, you know how exhilarating it can be when you finally reach the summit. Mountains have a special way of lifting us above the ordinary and allowing us to survey our world from a new and exciting perspective. It's different up there. All the mediocrity seems to drop away, and in the clean air we can breathe deeply a world that's fresher and more spiritually connected, where we can rise above the routine and feel our hearts swell with the thrill of achievement.

For obvious reasons, some people will never have a mountaintop experience, because it requires both planning and an intention to start climbing. These are perhaps the same people who believe that everything they desire should be handed to them with no effort on their part. They buy a lottery ticket and sit back and wait for the big moment. And despite that famous lottery slogan, "Hey, you never know," their moment rarely ever comes. Meanwhile, time slips by and life goes on.

Climbing mountains and achieving our dreams have a lot in common: they both require us to step outside our comfort zone.

The idea of the comfort zone goes back to one renowned experiment. In 1908, psychologists John D. Dodson and Robert M. Yerkes explained that a state of relative comfort creates a steady level of performance. In order to maximize performance, we need to be in a state of relative anxiety – where our stress levels are slightly higher than normal. This state is called "optimal anxiety," and it's just outside our comfort zone.

Some of the benefits of pushing yourself to step outside your comfort zone:

- You'll be more productive. Without the sense of unease that comes from having deadlines and expectations, we tend to just do what is necessary to get by and we lose the ambition to do more and learn new things. We also use the excuse that we're busy as a way to stay in our comfort zone and avoid trying new things.
- Choosing to live outside your comfort zone on occasion

can help prepare for dealing with unexpected changes that force you out of it. Fear and uncertainty are natural, but by taking risks in a controlled way and challenging yourself to things you normally wouldn't do, you can have a practice feeling a little bit uncomfortable.

- Once you start stepping outside your comfort zone, the zone itself gets bigger, and the easier it becomes to push your boundaries in new and different ways.
- You'll also find it easier to harness your creativity. Seeking new experiences and learning new skills opens the door to innovation. A positively uncomfortable experience can help us see old problems from a different perspective and tackle the challenges we face with renewed enthusiasm.

Those who have been to the mountaintop know that it takes effort to get there, but once you've been, you can't wait to challenge yourself to reach the next peak, even if it means more discomfort and more hard work.

CHAPTER 5

THE BEGINNINGS ARE HUMBLE AND NOT VERY SEXY

If you attended Vancouver's Pacific National Exhibition some 43 years ago, you might have purchased a hotdog from the "Footlong Hotdog" stand. That was my humble but not very sexy beginning as an entrepreneur.

This year, Canada Wide Media celebrates 40 years in business. In my 50 or 60 annual speaking engagements, it always amazes me how often I'm asked how I got started in business. I guess people are intrigued as to what steps an entrepreneur needs to take to get off the ground. Again, let me stress that, in the beginning, it's the furthest thing from glamourous.

Some 40-plus years ago, my wife needed a car. I was in

sales at the *Columbian Newspaper*; at the time, it was the oldest daily publication in the province, but my income did not allow for a second car.

The Pacific National Exhibition (or PNE) is held each year the last 17 days in August and attracts almost a million visitors. I heard about a business opportunity to own a stand there selling "foot-long" hotdogs. I thought, "Seventeen days? This would be a breeze." So I bought the hotdog stand with the goal of buying a car for Kay. The real question: who was going to run the hotdog stand? The answer: Kay. However I had to buy the car so she could get to work, which was at the fairgrounds about 40 minutes from our house. So we paid about $450 for an old English car, an Austin 1100. It had to be reliable transportation if it was made in our homeland of England!

The opening day of the fair, the entire family – Kay, my parents and my daughter Samantha – were there selling footlong hotdogs at the PNE. It was a beautiful day, fair attendance was very high and we were feeling optimistic. We had exceptional sales that very first day, but it poured rain the next 16 days straight, and I'm sure most of the modest profits we made were offset by all of the hotdogs young Samantha gobbled up. At the end of the fair, we had barely broken even, but we paid all our bills, we still owned the car and we learned some valuable, life-changing lessons.

Most businesses have similarly humble beginnings,

and to be successful over the long term requires a strong constitution, firm commitment and persistence. No two years are the same and there are always challenges, even when you've been around for 40 years, like Canada Wide Media. Norman Vincent Peale once said, "The only people without problems are in a cemetery." I would agree.

CHAPTER 6

DON'T MAJOR IN THE MINORS

According to the human resources experts at Robert Half International, the average employee works only 50 per cent of the time they are at work. The other 50 per cent is largely wasted on idle chit-chat with co-workers, late arrivals, extended coffee breaks and lunches, early departures, private phone calls, Internet surfing, checking email and other personal business.

"Don't major in the minors," my dad always told me. "Do the tough things first and take control of both your career and your future."

It's good advice and I would also add the following: Resolve to work all of the time that you are at work. If you are finding it difficult, try giving yourself a little reminder like "back on track" each time that you realize you've gotten distracted from what you need to be doing.

Contrary to what some experts will tell you, there is no magic formula when it comes to getting the hard work done or reaching your goals. If you wait around for inspiration to get you going, you might be waiting for a long time. A much more practical approach, and the one that has worked for me, is to methodically work towards your goals. If you want to know how effective what you are doing is, break your work day down into every action and ask yourself this question: "Will what I am doing right now take me toward my goals or away from them?"

If you're hanging around the watercooler talking about last night's crop of reality shows or trading gossip, I think you know the answer.

We do not manage time.

We can only manage ourselves.

Choose to make the most of every minute.

It's more of a mental game than anything else. While tips can be helpful, if we're just looking for an easy fix, chances are it's going to become another distraction that keeps us from focusing on what we really need to accomplish.

CHAPTER 7

WHY FAILURE IS GOOD FOR YOU

I'm sure somebody at some point in your life has told you to embrace your failures. Most likely, you just shook your head and asked, "Why would I want to do that?" Or maybe you thought to yourself, "That's easy for them to say, they don't have to live with it, I do." And you're absolutely right, but here's what's so good about that.

Failure does not prevent success. Just the opposite, in fact. By accepting that something has failed and moving on, you'll be able to focus on alternatives that might just be a better fit for you.

1. Accept that you're human and get over the guilt.
Everybody fails. They may not all advertise those failures, but

trust me, even the people who seem to go from one success to another have had their share o failures. Guilt, shame, embarrassment – these are only helpful in so much as they help you identify the lessons that can be learned so you can move on and try something else.

2. Talk it out.

"Find a shoulder to cry on, but not just any shoulder," is the advice from blogger Lewis Schiff, who wrote the book *Business Brilliant*. "Most people don't want to talk about failure because they are ashamed of it," explains Schiff. Which is exactly why you are unlikely to get helpful support and insights from people who haven't faced similar challenges; and that includes family and close friends. There are some things that only others in the same situation can understand, so it's better to seek out someone who has been there and done that.

3. Be honest with yourself.

Once a deal or project falls apart, own up to what went wrong. Start all the way at the beginning. The acute failures that killed the project right at the end might have only been symptoms of chronic problems that were there from the beginning and just continued to grow. Maybe you were working with the wrong client, in the wrong market or with the wrong team. The real lesson might be about choosing who you work with and the projects you work on more carefully, not about details of the execution that went badly.

4. Own it.
Don't go looking for others to blame when one of your endeavours goes off the rails, even though they may have had some part to play. Look first at yourself. Did you communicate your expectations clearly? Perhaps you avoided asking difficult questions because you just wanted to close the deal. Or maybe you didn't take the time to find out what was really needed. It's easy to blame others when things go wrong, but you can't control others; so assume they will remain the same and you're the one who must learn and adjust if you want the next project to be more successful.

5. Dust yourself off and try again.
Once you've figured out what you can learn from your failure, it's time to get back in the game. Your second attempt at something is always stronger than your first. You're older and wiser than you were before and you know a few things to look out for. Use that to your advantage.

CHAPTER 8

THE MOST SUCCESSFUL FAILURE IN THE WORLD

"One thing is certain in business: You and everyone around you will make mistakes." — Richard Branson

Most know Richard Branson as an iconic, daring entrepreneur – a self-made billionaire who challenged established businesses by providing better services and products to consumers. It wasn't always this way.

When he was a child, Branson struggled with dyslexia and as a result, he didn't do well in school. In fact, on his last day, his headmaster told him he would either end up in prison or become a millionaire.

But he wasn't successful in life just because he had a chip on his shoulder; it was because he refused to let failure keep him from moving forward. So when Branson failed, he simply got back at it and tried again. Here's a list of some of his failed ventures: Virgin Cola, Virgin Clothes, Virgin Money, Virgin Jeans, Virgin Vision, Virgin Vodka, Virgin Wine, Virgin Brides, Virgin Cosmetics and Virgin Cars.

The important lesson in all of this for other entrepreneurs is to be resilient, persistent and willing to learn from mistakes. These are the traits that have made Sir Richard Branson one of the most successful businessmen in the world.

Some of Branson's best advice: "Do not be embarrassed by your failures, learn from them and start again."

CHAPTER 9

ALWAYS HAVE A GOAL TO WORK ON

We can't control everything about our lives – interest rates, the economy, the price of housing, the job market – but working towards a goal gives us something positive to focus on and lays the foundation for future success. If you aren't building towards something, you're probably stagnating and when that happens you can start to feel like a victim, trapped by your own life. The best way to reverse that is to work towards a goal.

No matter what your passion is, get out there and start doing something. As Lao Tzu said, even a journey of a thousand miles begins with a single step.

Today, choose one thing that you've always wanted to do. It might be something from your bucket list, like skydiving or climbing a mountain; or it could be learning a new language or upgrading your education; or perhaps it involves giving back to the community through volunteer work or social activism. Whatever your ambition is, put it in writing and then come up with one tangible step that you can take right now to set you on your way.

Having a sense of purpose and an exciting goal to work towards makes everything you do feel more meaningful and it gives you more control over your life.

Take the first step on a new journey today.

As Henry Ford once remarked: "Before anything else, getting ready is the secret of success."

CHAPTER 10

WHAT I LEARNED FROM JACK

I n 2006, my company produced the official program for the Telus Skins golf tournament, which was held at the Nicklaus North golf course in Whistler, B.C. During the tournament, my wife Kay and I had the opportunity to walk in the crowd following legendary PGA champion Jack Nicklaus.

As he prepared to take his second shot on the 12th hole, Nicklaus turned to his caddie and asked, "How far to the green?" Glancing down the fairway, his caddie responded, "About 91 or 92 yards." Jack quickly turned to him and said, "Well, which is it, 91 or 92 yards?"

Talk about precision.

Thinking about it later, I realized that while that one yard wouldn't make much difference to you or me, Jack's entire career as a champion was built on his ability to get the ball as close to the pin as possible. In his world, one yard could be the difference between sinking that all-important putt to win the tournament or having to take another stroke and end up finishing out of the money. There's a reason that golf courses all over the world are named after Jack.

There are times in all of our lives when we need to perform like a champion, where "close enough" just isn't good enough and we have to be more, do more and deliver more than the competition to be successful. At those moments, we need to be ready to step up and get in the game.

If you want to be a champion, you have to be on top of your game. Here are some tips from Jack that I think apply to much more than just golf:

1. *As a general rule, the rough does strange things to golfers. They stop thinking. Even experienced club players try to pull off circus shots they would never dream of hitting from a fairway lie.*

2. *A healthy, if well-concealed, respect for one's own capabilities is essential, but it should never lead to underestimating those of the opponent.*

3. *Once the gun has gone off, you keep quiet and get on with the job as best you can. The more you let your mind dwell on negatives, of whatever type, the larger they grow and the*

greater the risk that you will convert them into excuses. I have preferred to save my energy for finding solutions to problematical conditions, rather than waste it on whining.

4. I would pinpoint four qualities that seem to be shared by all consistent winners: the ability to think clearly under pressure, patience, self-centredness (concern about what other competitors may or may not be doing is both a useless distraction and a waste of energy) and simply working harder at all of the above when you are playing poorly.

5. Whether admitted or not, every successful person has a hard time with ego. When you have excelled in one area, it becomes all too easy to believe you will automatically do equally well at anything else you try.

CHAPTER 11

DO IT ANYWAY

T he following poem, originally written by a Harvard undergrad named Kent M. Keith in 1968, was found on the wall of Shishu Bhavan, the children's home in Calcutta supported by Mother Teresa:

People are unreasonable, illogical and self-centred.
LOVE THEM ANYWAY

If you do good, people will accuse you of selfish, ulterior motives.
DO GOOD ANYWAY

If you are successful, you will win false friends and true enemies.
SUCCEED ANYWAY

The good you do will be forgotten tomorrow.
DO IT ANYWAY

Honesty and frankness make you vulnerable.
BE HONEST AND FRANK ANYWAY

What you spend years building may be destroyed overnight.
BUILD ANYWAY

People really need help but may attack you if you help them.
HELP PEOPLE ANYWAY

Give the world the best you have and you'll get kicked in the teeth.
GIVE THE WORLD THE BEST YOU'VE GOT ANYWAY

> **"We ourselves feel that what we are doing is just a drop in the ocean. But the ocean would be less because of that missing drop."** —*MOTHER TERESA*

Mother Teresa dedicated her life to helping others without any expectations about what she would receive in return. It's not a bad philosophy for the rest of us as we pursue our many dreams. Take these eight principles and apply them to your life, your career, your family and your community and you will discover that this wisdom will move you from success to significance.

CHAPTER 12

ALL IN A WEEK'S WORK!

In late 2015, I spent a week in the Deep South on a speaking tour in Mobile, Alabama. It was my first time in that part of the world; I was there speaking to employees of Phantom Screens, which is headquartered in Abbotsford, B.C.

Day 1: I took two American Airlines flights to get there safe and sound.

I checked into the Battle House Renaissance Hotel, which was established in 1851. As I walked into the hotel lobby, a sign shining on the entrance greeted me with, "What inspires you?" I decided to incorporate that question into the three presentations I was slated to give, altering it to: "Who inspires you and why?"

Day 2: Most of the office buildings and stores in downtown Mobile are vacant, partially due to the 2008 recession, but nobody was negative about it, since efforts were already underway to rejuvenate business in the centre of the city.

A block from my hotel (and just a half block from historic Bienville Square), I found downtown Mobile's best bookstore. It contained thousands of historic hardcover books – rare first editions on history, military, classics, local art and furnishings, all set out on two spacious floors. I needed more time to explore than I had but I felt obliged to add to my collection of "quote" books and bought Kathryn and Ross Petras's *Don't Forget to Sing in the Lifeboats*; 300 pages of inspiring words from great thinkers, and it only cost $1.

This one quote by the English writer A.A. Milne caught my attention:

"Rivers know this: There is no hurry. We shall get there some day."

Day 3: I had lunch in the Joe Cain Cafe. He lived from 1832 to 1904 and was responsible, along with other societies and organizations in Mobile, for developing Mardi Gras parades; a few years later, following the Civil War, they moved the party to New Orleans.

Day 4: Esther De Wolde, CEO of Phantom Screens, had a big dream of buying an old Southern home in Mobile, Alabama, and restoring it to its former beauty.

She purchased the Morgan-Ford House, which was established in 1906, and did just that. The house is called "Southern Romance" and is located at 257 Rapier Avenue. Esther had a reception in the tented lot next to the house and all the delegates in town for this event had an opportunity to visit the beautiful home, which is completely restored along with priceless antiques, photos and paintings.

Esther turned something old into something new: her dream complete.

What is your big dream and how are you doing with it?

As Desmond Tutu once said: "Dream! Dream! And then go for it!"

Day 5: Presentation day to all the delegates at the Battle House Hotel.

The highlight for me, being that it was November 11, Remembrance Day, was Esther's interview with 93-year-old Miss Kathryn. She and her late husband, who served his country in Hawaii, were both personal witnesses to the attack on Pearl Harbor on December 7, 1941.

Miss Kathryn's memory was clear and she spoke with great passion about her country, conveying the tremendous shock and devastation of actually seeing this surprise attack. Her faculties were 100 per cent – making her a living legacy of an important time in her U.S. history.

Day 6: Time to leave Mobile for an hour-and-a-half plane ride to Dallas/Fort Worth and spend the night at the Hyatt Hotel at the Dallas/Fort Worth International Airport (DFW). I arrive about 11 p.m. and think I've found the hotel but nobody has told me there are two Hyatt Hotels at DFW. Did they ever think of changing one of the names? Together with four other weary travellers, I find a minibus to transfer us to the other hotel – a full hour later.

Day 7: Final flight home – American Airlines, Flight #1167. We board and are ready to leave on time with the pilot in place, but no co-pilot. It turns out he's on a 45-minute delayed flight from Tampa and landed at the "other" Terminal at DFW. So, a two-and-a-half hour trip stretches out to four hours.

My week in a nutshell: tired, inspired, fulfilled and full of adventure. That's the life of a speaker and I love it!

CHAPTER 13

DON'T GET UPSET BUT . . .
YOU'RE DOING IT ALL WRONG

I read an article recently titled "Don't Get Upset But Exercising Doesn't Make You Lose Weight." It addressed the common misconception that if you want to lose weight, all you need to do is exercise more and get your metabolism revved up to burn more calories. Sounds like good common-sense advice, right? The flaw in the plan is that exercising does make you burn more calories, but it also makes you feel hungry because you're burning more calories. Most people overestimate how many calories they've actually burned from exercise, so they feel justified in eating more and as a result, they fail to lose weight and eventually become discouraged.

In order to actually lose weight, we have to adjust both our level of physical activity and our eating habits: exercising more and eating less (not to mention healthier) food.

I've struggled with maintaining a healthy weight for most of my adult life and despite yo-yoing up and down, I've never really questioned the logic of the diet and exercise advice I received.

But sometimes the right way to do things is counter-intuitive to accepted wisdom. If you're not getting the results you want – whether it be in your health, career or personal relationships – stop repeating the same thing over and over. Try something different. Ask others what's worked for them, scour the Internet for new ideas, check out the latest research, shake it up!

Here are a few other things you might be doing wrong, but didn't know it:

Brushing your teeth after you eat – Turns out, acidic foods or drinks soften tooth enamel and brushing right after you eat strips enamel from the teeth, leaving them vulnerable to cavities. This is particularly true for children. The best time to brush your teeth is actually before you eat and flossing is a better option for removing bits of food from your teeth after a meal.

Leaving the roof racks or bike racks on your vehicle –

Researchers at the National Renewable Energy Laboratory in Berkeley found that these type of accessories attached to the exterior of a vehicle can increase aerodynamic drag on your vehicle by as much as 25 per cent. If you're not using them all the time, take them off and save some money on fuel – as well as decrease your environmental footprint.

Showering or bathing every day – You probably didn't know you have a protective layer on the outside of your skin called the stratum corneum (or "horny layer"); much less that it protects you from infection and disease and is damaged every time you bathe or shower, particularly if you use hot water, soap or any type of exfoliating device.

Skipping a shower now and then gives your skin time to repair and replace the horny layer – and have no fear, it won't make you any dirtier. Studies have shown there is no measurable difference in the number of microorganism colonies a person is host to regardless of how frequently they shower. Air drying is also better than using a towel to dry off, as it keeps the horny layer intact.

You don't know your net worth – A lot of people think they're doing well financially if they can make payments on the things they want and manage to pay their bills every month, which can lead to thinking it's OK to take out huge loans for things like cars that they can't actually afford. In order to see the full picture of your financial situation, you need to focus on your net worth (all of your assets minus any money you owe). Once you have your net worth, it's easy to calculate whether the things you're pouring money into are helping you get further ahead (like investments and savings) or go further into debt (like depreciating assets such as cars, electronics or toys).

Trying to maintain a "normal" sleep schedule – Experts are always touting the importance of getting enough sleep and going to bed earlier, but many people who try to control their sleep actually find they're more exhausted than ever. The old adage, "early to bed, early to rise" may work for some, but it sure doesn't feel that way for everyone. So, instead of conforming to the old notions of what normal sleep is, experiment to find what works for you and your body. For example, if you feel like you're the most productive during the wee hours of the morning, take a nap earlier in the evening, wake up, then take another nap at some point during the day to make up the number of hours that are optimal for you. Not everyone requires the same amount of sleep.

To figure out what's right for you, Dr. Michael Breus, an insomnia expert, recommends going to bed seven-and-a-half hours before you want to wake up and then adjusting your sleep schedule by 15 minutes (up or down) based on how you feel, until you find the magic number.

CHAPTER 14

ALL YOU HAVE TO DO IS *ASK*

I love sales and the art of selling and I really do think it is an art. I love it almost as much as giving a good speech. The two have a lot in common: a motivating speech sells your ideas and moves people to take action in their own lives, while a well-crafted sales pitch moves people to buy your products.

It always amazes me how reluctant even veteran salespeople are to ask the client to buy.

I've heard statistics that 50 per cent to 90 per cent of salespeople simply never get around to asking the buyer for the order. Very often, in a casual way, I might ask for the sale before I even sit to discuss the details. People are afraid to ask the question because they are afraid of rejection, which they believe is personal as opposed to not having explained your product and its benefits adequately.

Case in point: if I'm attempting to sell you a series of four colour ads in *BCBusiness* magazine, I could begin the conversation with, "Your ad would look great in full colour on page three." That is a very soft closing technique and the client's response to that will give me an idea of their mindset.

You don't have to be formal. Use phrases like "Why don't we just proceed?" or "Let's just do this deal."

A more formal approach might be, "Why don't I write up the contract and get the formalities out of the way?"

Sometimes, if I feel like the sales interview is going off-track, I might say to the client, "Can you give me one example of what might have caused you to say "Yes" today?" Nine times out of 10, the client will tell you what stopped them from going forward with the deal. Then you need to figure out if you can resolve that problem. Or, you could repeat back to the client what that obstacle is: "So what you're telling me is, if I could remove this obstacle, you would proceed with this purchase?" They will either tell you "yes" or "no", and if it's "no", then it wasn't the real problem to begin with and you have to drill down further to find out what the issue is.

Even if you aren't a salesperson per se, everyone should know how to ask for what they want, because as the old saying goes, "If you don't ask, you don't get." People who speak up are also more likely to get promoted, no matter what role they're going after because leaders want to know that you've got the guts to ask for what you want as well as the self-confidence and determination to convince them to give it to you.

If you're interested in honing your sales skills, I suggest you look at the online Professional Selling Skills Program, offered by Ralph Kison through the Peter Legge International Institute for Sales Excellence at Douglas College. Th course is designed to equip those new to selling, and even experienced sellers, with the resources to refine and update their approach and techniques to achieve the highest levels of professionalism and sales excellence.

Nothing happens until somebody sells something!

CHAPTER 15

TAKE A HIKE

A recent article in *Condé Nast Traveler* talks about how hiking can actually change our brain. "From lessening negativity to boosting creativity, hiking in fresh air actually boosts brain power and can help certain parts of the brain grow," writes Meredith Carey, who outlines three brain benefits.

The first is our ability to problem solve. Being in the outdoors and away from the distractions of technology can raise cognitive function by as much as 50 per cent, resulting in better problem solving and more creative thinking.

The second benefit is related to memory. Studies show that walking in nature impacts the hippocampus, which is the brain's memory hub and can help stave off Alzheimer's and other memory-related illnesses. Some countries in Europe have gone so far as to recommend to citizens that they get a minimum dose of five hours of nature per month to improve mental health and memory.

Finally, hiking helps to cut down on negativity. Studies at Stanford University found that walking in nature helps to reduce blood flow in the subgenual prefrontal cortex (the area of the brain associated with negative thinking) and eliminate the obsessive and negative thoughts that we all experience from time to time, particularly when we are brooding about something. So not only does a walk or hike provide you with physical exercise, it also benefits your brain and your mood.

CHAPTER 16

HAVE YOU REACHED YOUR EVEREST?

At the time I was researching and writing my second book, I was also on the board of Variety Clubs International, which was meeting in Vancouver to choose the humanitarian award winner for that year. The award is the highest honour that Variety can bestow on an individual. Previous recipients had included Sir Winston Churchill, Bob Hope and Princess Anne.

The annual convention where the award would be presented was taking place in New Zealand that year and the candidate who stood out from all the rest was that country's own Sir Edmund Hillary. From every angle, he was a giant, deserving of the highest praise and admiration.

I was in my mid-teens when Sir Edmond became the first person to climb Mount Everest, and for me, like many young people at the time, he was an instant hero.

Many people believe that it is quite possible Edmund Hillary was not the first to summit Everest – the explorer George Mallory may have reached the peak 30 years earlier, although the truth remains a mystery even today. The reason we know Hillary's name and not Mallory's is that Hillary not only made it to the peak, he also made it back down. Mallory did not – he lost his life on that mountain.

Climbing up is one thing, but many have found coming back down to be fatal.

In an interview, Sir Edmund was asked to name the biggest challenge he faced in becoming the first man to successfully scale Everest. The biggest obstacle, he responded, was a psychological one – he had to constantly find ways to keep from talking himself out of it.

In climbing the mountain, he not only showed the world it could be done; most importantly, he showed himself.

"It was not the mountain we conquered that day," he is famous for saying. "It was ourselves."

My takeaway from this is that it's easy to talk ourselves out of going after what we want or to think that it takes someone with talents and abilities far greater than our own to accomplish something of significance; these are the things we must overcome. As Hillary himself said, "In some ways, I believe I epitomize the average New Zealander: I have modest abilities, I combine these with a good deal of determination and I rather like to succeed."

How about you, have you reached your Everest?

CHAPTER 17

GIVE IT ALL YOU'VE GOT

During the 1988 Winter Olympics in Calgary, there was a 25-year-old Swiss skier by the name of Pirman Zurbriggen. He was competing in the combined alpine skiing event, which consists of one downhill race plus two slalom runs, with all times added together for a combined total.

Zurbriggen was considered to be one of the all-time greatest skiers. For this particular race, he simply had to finish (not win) his final run and the gold medal would be his.

Imagine: a gold medal, all the adoration, all the glory!

Zurbriggen exploded out of the gate, but two thirds of the way down the mountain, he caught an edge and fell – no gold medal. I wonder what others would have done. If it were me, with so much at stake, I'd have skied that race *very* carefully.

At the bottom of the hill, dozens of reporters, in every language imaginable, asked him, "Why? Why did you not take your time and just complete the run??"

Zurbriggen said nothing; he just walked away.

Sometime later, at Copper Mountain, a ski resort just outside of Denver, one of my speaking associates, Mark Sanborn, was riding on the lift next to Zurbriggen's ski instructor and personal friend.

Sanborn had seen all the important races at the 1988 Winter Olympics and just had to ask, why would Pirman Zurbriggen risk it? Why would he risk a gold medal?

The instructor said, "In my opinion, he was always trying to ski his best race, no matter what." It wasn't just about the medal, he wanted to pursue his potential.

Although he retired from international competition in 1990, Zurbriggen remains one of the best to ever compete in alpine skiing.

None of us really knows how good we *could* be and no one really knows how good our companies *could* be.

As Shakespeare wrote, "We know what we are, but not what we may be."

Sometimes, in our day-to-day activities in pursuit of success – with our families, in our sports, in serving the community and in our businesses – we're reluctant to give it 100 per cent, even when there's no Olympic gold medal at stake. But life is shorter than you think, so give it all you've got.

CHAPTER 18

LESSONS LEARNED THE HARD WAY

"Maybe you needed to get whacked hard by life before you understood what you wanted out of it." —Jodi Picoult

L ife's crossroads, despite the difficulties they present, create opportunities for change. The choices we make can either help us grow and improve, or stifle us and knock us down. The life lessons we learn during times of hardship are 10 times more abundant than those we pick up when things are going our way, but even though they may be hard to swallow, that doesn't mean they aren't valuable. Here are a few of the lessons I learned the hard way:

Things are never as bad as they seem.

Bad things happen to good people; in fact, they happen to everyone, and usually for no particular reason. After I had my stroke, part of my body was paralyzed and I struggled to see how I would ever recover. I couldn't imagine a life where I was unable to be a speaker – it was the thing I loved to do most in the world.

Eventually, I had to accept that my recovery might be slow and it was going to take a lot of hard work. I also came to realize that it is the person who is able to put things into the proper perspective and get on with life that eventually succeeds, even if life ends up looking quite different from what it once was. When you have been through a tough time or two, you start to realize that you are more resilient than you thought and no matter what happens, you can, and will, go on.

Life's too unpredictable for rigid expectations.

When you stop expecting things to be a certain way, you can appreciate them for what they are. Life's greatest gifts are rarely wrapped the way you expected them to be, but with a positive attitude and an open mind, you will find that even though things don't always happen when and how you expect, that isn't a bad thing; it's actually what makes life interesting.

It never hurts to ask.
When your best friend asks out the person of your dreams and they say "yes", you will regret not voicing your interest. When someone gets the promotion you wanted, you will regret not asking for it first. And when someone breaks your heart, you will regret not asking why. Life is short and opportunity doesn't like to wait around. Not asking for what you want is far more painful in the long run than overcoming the fear of rejection – but you probably won't fully appreciate this wisdom until you watch what you want slip away, or worse yet, go to someone else.

You don't have to live your life the way others expect you to.
Your work is going to fill a large part of your life and the only way to be truly satisfied is to do what you believe is great work –

> "The difference between school and life? In school, you're taught a lesson and then given a test. In life, you're given a test that teaches you a lesson." —TOM BODETT

which means you need to love what you do. If you haven't found it yet, keep looking. Don't settle. As with all matters of the heart, you'll know when you find it. So keep looking and don't be afraid to go in a new direction. Life is so much easier when you live it for yourself.

Don't wait.

The older you get, the more complicated life is and the less likely you are to spontaneously do the things you dream about. It is easier to travel, experiment and take risks when you're younger and have fewer responsibilities. It's also easier to recover from a mistake and apply the valuable life lessons those mistakes provide, so jump to it!

It takes consistent effort and practice to become an expert.

There is no elevator to success; you have to take the stairs. People usually get discouraged when it takes more time than they thought to master a skill or climb the ladder of success within their chosen career. Having a university degree doesn't make you an expert, you need to pay your dues. As Malcom Gladwell theorized in his book *Outliers*, on average it takes 10,000 hours of practice to truly master a skill, so there's no time to waste. Get a move on!

CHAPTER 19

TO BE SUCCESSFUL,
YOU HAVE TO SACRIFICE

About a year ago, the University of Victoria honoured 16-time Grammy Award winner David Foster with its annual Distinguished Entrepreneur Award at a gala at the Empress Hotel in Victoria.

The Victoria-born Foster was keen to accept this unique honour, but was asked to give a 20-minute speech. The whole thing almost went off track when David responded to the request by saying, "I can't and won't speak for 20 minutes . . . but why don't you get my friend Peter Legge to interview me instead?"

Pat Elemans, assistant dean of the Peter B. Gustavson School of Business, called and asked me if I would come to the gala in Victoria and do the interview; if I agreed, she would fly me down to Malibu, California, to David's magnificent home, where we would work out the questions. Of course I said, "Yes, absolutely!"

Prior to the awards gala, David opened himself up to the packed University of Victoria lecture hall, answering questions such as, "What is the most important key to success?" His answer: "Networking – two minds are better than one." David also told the students, "Good is the enemy of great," explaining that he has known people who could have been great, but stalled at good. He added that if you're not working on Saturday or Sunday, somebody else is. On top of all that, he shared that he doesn't believe in luck. To David's way of thinking, "Luck is when hard work meets opportunity."

At the event, one young lady in the audience spoke up and shared that she manages her sister's music career. "If you could hear my sister sing and play piano, you might record her," she said to David.

David immediately shot back, "Where does your sister live?"

> "Success is no accident. It is hard work, perseverance, learning, studying, sacrifice and most of all, love of what you are doing or learning to do." —*PELE*

"She lives in Toronto," the young woman answered.

"How long have you known I was going to be here?" he asked.

"Since about five days ago," was her reply.

"Well then, you should have flown her out from Toronto last night on a low-cost red eye and your sister and I could have met in person – who knows what might have happened. Next time, bring your sister or get her another manager!"

"You must learn to sacrifice in this business if you want to get ahead," he advised the audience.

I'd say that's some pretty solid advice if you're an aspiring talent; it's not every day that you're going to get the opportunity to put yourself in the same room as an award-winning producer like David Foster.

So let me ask you: Whatever your business or your dream is, are you giving it 100 per cent?

What are you prepared to give up in order to make it?

To be successful at any venture, sacrifice is essential.

You have to sacrifice to be great. Period.

CHAPTER 20

WHAT'S STOPPING YOU?

My father Bernie Legge always told me, "Don't accept success or failure – neither need be permanent."

Success does not guarantee continued success. You must keep working at it and growing and learning as an individual.

Eighty per cent of the professional speakers who were in the business 10 years ago are no longer in the business today. Perhaps they forgot to keep reading, studying, learning from others, improving on their skills, rehearsing, and most significantly, they've forgotten how to answer the three important questions that I ask every aspiring speaker who approaches me for advice:

1. What do you want to speak about that makes you worth listening to?

2. Who will pay you for this?

3. How will they find out about you?

One of the reasons I love what I do so much is that there are always new opportunities and challenges to help me get better at it. When the Olympics came to Vancouver, I set my sights on getting hired to emcee the opening ceremonies. Although things didn't turn out *exactly* as I expected, I was thrilled to be the only speaker contracted to give a motivational speech at the Olympics – I delivered my speech at the very first victory ceremony in BC Place Stadium and it was an experience I will never forget.

There are a lot of experiences that could potentially crush our dreams, but only if we let them. More often than not, it isn't the external things that keep us from moving on, it's the stuff that's going on inside, such as:

- Failing to address damaging beliefs and mindsets.
- Not recognizing and believing in your own special talents, abilities and gifts.
- Neglecting to embrace and uplift others along the way, and build a true support community.
- Letting a lack of courage and confidence stop you.
- Not building the boundaries that are necessary to protect you and your ideas.
- Not committing deeply enough to what you want to accomplish.

- Constantly looking to others for validation and recognition.

Quit running around trying to find a quick fix. Just stop, breathe deeply and take a good long look at yourself.

Blogger Chris Guillebeau talks about how his choice to become a "travel hacker" (someone who travels the world without spending much money in the process) meant that he had to make choices about what's important to him. Between 2002 and 2013, Chris visited every country in the world. To achieve his dream, he chose not to have a car or a house; instead he took transit or rode his bike and he rented an apartment so that he could dedicate his money to travel. He also doesn't have a "job"; instead, he earns his income from products and services offered through his website and blog, *The Art of Non-Conformity*.

When Chris (who calls Portland, Oregon home) travels, the people he meets are always fascinated by his lifestyle and invariably say something to the effect of, "That sounds amazing, I wish I could do that."

His response: "What's keeping you from it?"

It's an excellent question and one that we should all ask when we find ourselves wishing we had something different than what we have or making rationalizations for why we aren't living our dreams.

Perhaps the most common reason for not taking action is: "I don't have the money to pursue my dream."

Chances are if you live in North America, you have more than enough money to meet your basic needs and plenty left over for the things that you want, such as your house or condo (complete with a big mortgage payment), a car (or two or three), a smartphone, cable television and high-speed Internet service, just to name a few recurring expenses that can add up very quickly.

The truth is that beyond basic food, shelter and transportation, everything else that we choose to spend our money on is exactly that, a choice – our choice. We choose what we value when we decide how to spend our time, money and other resources.

Are you willing to sacrifice your dreams in order to live the life you have or are you willing to sacrifice a few comforts and do what it takes to live your dream? Here are two questions that Chris suggests people ask themselves to help determine if they are on the right path to fulfilling their dreams:

1. Am I satisfied with my job and career?

Your job should do more than simply provide income for the rest of your life. Ask yourself, "Am I working to make a living or to make a life?" If your work supports your goals, that's great. If it doesn't, maybe it's time to change.

2. What are my financial priorities?

If you have difficulty answering this one, there's an easy way to tell. Check your credit card statements for the past six months. Where you've been spending your money is where your priorities are.

Once you fully understand what you want, it's usually not difficult to get it.

Chris's advice for dealing with critics and naysayers? "At all stages of life, people will gladly offer you unsolicited lists of things you 'must' do, be or have. Most of the time you can nod your head, walk away and ignore them."

The life you have is the one you've made for yourself. If you want something different, you're going to have to do something differently.

PART 2

THE COURAGE OF LEADERSHIP

*Leadership is all about influence and everything
rises and falls on leadership . . . everything.*
—John C. Maxwell

CHAPTER 21

MANAGEMENT IS DOING THINGS RIGHT. LEADERSHIP IS DOING THE RIGHT THINGS.

"If your actions inspire others to dream more, learn more, do more and become more, you are a leader." —John Quincy Adams

As I write this, the 27th year of the **BCBusiness Top 100 Luncheon** is just over a month away. This premier event is the largest networking opportunity in Vancouver and has attracted approximately 1,300 business leaders every year to the Fairmont Hotel Vancouver.

As I mentioned earlier, the special guests featured at the

luncheon during these past five years have been stellar –
billionaire Jimmy Pattison; my mentor of 50 years Joe Segal;
businessman Frank Giustra; Vancouver Canucks owner
Francesco Aquilini, and last year, Cactus Club Cafe founder
Richard Jaffray.

All of them truly are strong and courageous leaders.
The stories they've told of achieving success from humble
beginnings, narrowly avoiding failure and the many struggles
they've overcome to reach the pinnacle of their respective
industries have been inspiring and thought-provoking.

This year it will be my pleasure to interview **Christine
Day.**

Christine was a Starbucks executive for 20 years and,
as employee No. 3 in the company, she worked directly
with CEO Howard Schultz. She is also the former CFO of
Lululemon in Vancouver and is now CEO of Luvo, a company
that produces nutritious frozen meals that are sourced and
packaged sustainably.

Christine's
remarkable career
is legendary and the
story of how she did
it is an inspiring one
... I just can't give it

> **"The most dangerous leadership myth is
> that leaders are born – that there is a genetic
> factor to leadership. That's nonsense;
> in fact, the opposite is true. Leaders are made
> rather than born." –WARREN BENNIS**

away here since I'm writing this before the event. What I will
say is that in all the years we have been doing this, the Top

100 Luncheon never disappoints.

As I noted a minute ago, Jim Pattison has also been one of our special guests. Jimmy is British Columbia's richest man. He's also among the top-10 richest men in Canada and the top-200 richest men in the world, according to *Forbes* magazine.

Although he may be a tough businessperson, in all the years that I've known Jimmy and done business with him, he's always been fair, honest and reliable. His word is good enough for me and the thousands of people he deals with. One thing everybody knows: he does exactly what he says he will, when he says he'll do it! You can count on Jim Pattison.

We purchased *BCBusiness* from him 25 years ago and my commitment to him was to make it the finest regional magazine in Canada. In 2014, we were presented with the Kenneth R. Wilson Award in Toronto as regional business magazine of the year in Canada. Jimmy was thrilled for us.

Something remarkable about Jimmy is that he has never worked for money – rather, he works to be successful. As a leader and a role model for others, he wants to be the best at what he does. It's a point of personal pride and it's something he admires in others.

During the Top 100 interview I did with Jimmy a few years back, he told the story of a visit he paid to one of his stores on Vancouver Island. As he walked through the aisles, he observed that the floor of the grocery store was absolutely spotless – he'd never seen such a shiny, clean, altogether immaculate floor.

He asked the store manager who was responsible for this. The manager's response: "The janitor."

"I need to meet him," Jimmy told the manager.

After complimenting the janitor on his exceptional work, Jimmy asked him, "How do you make the floors look so impeccably clean?"

Not realizing who he was talking to, the man simply replied, "I don't listen to head office."

At this point in the story, Jimmy turned to the 1,300-person audience and said, "Every one of you in this audience can do something unique and better than anyone else. Find that one thing and do it."

And that, I believe, is the secret to success in life and something that all of our Top 100 guests have in common. They all found that "one thing" they could do better than anyone else and because they had the courage to do something about it, they became successful leaders.

Henry Ford once said, "The whole secret of a successful life is to find out what it is one's destiny to do, and then do it."

Leadership takes courage. Aristotle called courage the first virtue, because it makes all of the other virtues possible.

Some of the stories and advice you'll find in this section of the book are old, some are new and some are simply timeless – all of it revolves around the courage of leadership.

CHAPTER 22

LESSONS ON LEADERSHIP

O
n January 15, 1942, the day after I was born, General George Patton arrived in Indio, California, to take command of a desert training centre. And while I came into the world with a gentle squawk, Patton rolled into town in a sirens-screaming motorcade.

Waiting expectantly for a traditional motivating speech, Patton's men watched him dismount his car at 11 a.m., the precise moment he was scheduled to take command. He saluted the troops and said: "I assume command of the First Armored Corps. At ease!"

Never one to pussyfoot around, Patton got right to the point. "We are at war with a tough enemy. We must train millions of men to be soldiers! We must make them tough in mind and body . . . We will start running from this point in exactly 30 minutes. I will lead!"

Good leaders inspire people to have confidence in their leadership. Great leaders inspire people to have confidence in themselves. If you plan to lead, you can't sit around waiting for something to happen. Leaders make bold moves. Leaders take risks. Leaders make use of their own ingenuity and do what has to be done. Even the best leaders make mistakes; it's how we move on from those mistakes that determines our success.

For 40 years, I have led Canada Wide Media in good times and bad through an ever-changing business climate. Our staff of 55 people produce over 25 quality products including magazines, trade publications and websites, making us the largest independently owned media publishing company in Western Canada.

What leadership skills do I use to propel Canada Wide forward year after year? I'm no General Patton, but I do have seven basic principles that I employ to assure the company's success:

Passion – You have to be excited about what you do, otherwise why do it at all?

Integrity – High moral values and a commitment to do the right thing will win the trust and loyalty of your team – two things you'll need to have to be an effective leader.

Energy/Enthusiasm/Excitement – It's contagious and it will carry you and your team through both the good and the bad.

Dedication to serve the community – We should never lose sight of the fact that we're all in this together; when our communities are strong and healthy, we all benefit.

Patience/Perseverance – Some days (or years) just aren't going to go the way you thought, but you have to hang in there.

Humility – Believe it or not, you don't know it all and neither do I. Listen to others and use their wisdom and experience to the benefit of your business.

Commitment to work hard and do the hard work – You need to love what you're doing because it's going to be hard work.

CHAPTER 23

LIFE BY THE NUMBERS

I had lunch with the MP from Port Moody, James Moore, shortly after he announced that he was leaving national politics. During our conversation, he talked about life and its length.

Eighty-five years equals 4,435 weeks.

Eighty-five years also equals 745,094 hours.

He told me that if I only have 12 years left in my life, I have 626 weeks or 105,190 hours remaining.

He told me it was something he had to consider every time he got on a plane for the 5-1/2 hour flight from Vancouver to Ottawa and again for the 6-1/2 hour flight back, which happened virtually every week while he was a member of parliament, because those were hours spent away from his wife and child. I think it's likely those numbers had some bearing on his decision to step down from Canadian national politics.

If you're familiar with my book *The Runway of Life*, you'll know this is a subject I've talked about before. If you're not, it's based on something my mentor Joe Segal said to me one day while we were having lunch.

"Many people think of life as a road or a highway," Joe told me. "But a highway can go on forever and life isn't like that. Life is more like a runway, because at some point you're going to run out of asphalt."

At this point in the conversation, Joe picked up a napkin off the table and drew a horizontal line across it. At the beginning of the line he put a zero and at the end of the line he put the number 90.

"That's how old I expect to be when I meet my maker," he said.

Next, Joe wrote his current age on the line and turned to me. "The part of the line between zero and your current age, that's history, it's done, so forget about it."

Then he pointed to the section of the line between his current age and where he expects his runway will end.

"This distance between where I am now and the end of my runway, that's all I've got to work with, so I have to ask myself, 'What am I going to do with the time that I have?' and whatever my answer is to that question, that's what I need to stay focused on."

Joe's simple runway exercise with the napkin struck a chord. I realized in that moment that none of us knows exactly how much time we have left and no matter what we have accomplished in the past – or how successful we have been – what really matters is the time we have ahead of us and what we choose to do with that time.

Something else to consider: life changes and we have to change too. My lunch conversation with James Moore is a perfect example. Moore was the youngest MP ever elected in British Columbia and I'm sure as a young, single, up-and-coming politician, flying to and from Ottawa on a weekly basis was exciting. However, as a husband and father with a young family, priorities shift; yet fear can keep us doing the same old things while time slips away.

> **"Most of us will not choose how we die. But we choose every day how we will live. Free will is a beautiful thing, yet it comes with responsibility and accountability. Only you can decide your fate through the priorities you set, the decisions you make, the efforts you spend, the sacrifices you make. What you choose for today will determine all of your tomorrows. Act accordingly!"** *—JOE SEGAL*

What do we fear the most? Here are the big ones that I came up with:

- Fear of change
- Fear of success
- Fear of failure

- Fear of losing status
- Fear of making a mistake

What we should be most afraid of is wasting time doing things that don't serve us – like procrastinating, doing work we aren't really passionate about, fighting with loved ones over things that don't really matter or wrestling with our conscience – rather than taking care of the things that are really important.

The real question to ask yourself is, "How much time can I afford to waste?"

If I were to ask you right now, "Do you want to waste your life?" I'm pretty confident you would say, "No, absolutely not!"

How about a decade?

Still no.

How about a year?

No again.

How about a month or a week?

No.

But how about a day?

Well, a day – big deal! Most people don't value a single day all on its own, because they think they have so many to spare.

Well, a day quickly becomes a week. A week becomes a month. Then a year. Before we know it, a decade has passed and soon we realize that we have more life behind us than before us – and we still haven't learned the value of a day and its importance to our entire life.

So, how much time are *you* willing to waste?

Whether we're doing the things that make us happy or not, the numbers quickly add up and the further we get along the runway, the faster we seem to be going. Time is one thing in our world that's definitely not recyclable, although I often wish it was. It's something to think about the next time you find yourself wasting time.

We are travelling inevitably towards the end of our lives — so seize today and make it count.

CHAPTER 24

WHAT WE'RE NOT

"You don't need to be elected to be a leader, you just need to step forward and help your family and community the best way you can. And being yourself is your best leadership style." —Kim Baird

In his book *Authentic Happiness*, Dr. Martin Seligman notes, "You cannot be anything you want to be – but you can be a lot more of who you already are."

Too many of us try too hard to be something we're not, or worse yet, we devote more time to fixing our shortcomings than developing our strengths. Sometimes we do it to please others, sometimes we do it because we think it will lead to wealth, fame or success. More often, it ends in depression, failure and disappointment.

Each of us is valuable because of the special talents that have been given to us, so why focus on what we're not?

A little over 10 years ago, the Gallup Organization (the global research company famous for the Gallup poll) developed a tool called the Strengths Finder to help people discover and develop their natural talents. Drawing on more than 40 years of research, they discovered the following basic truths about human achievement and success:

- A life spent focusing on improving our weaknesses leads to dissatisfaction and mediocrity.
- Spending time doing what we love and are best at is what drives success.
- We cannot be great at everything, so we need to acknowledge our limitations, build on our strengths and get on with life.

> "Very few people do this anymore. It's too risky. First of all, it's a hell of a responsibility to be yourself. It's much easier to be somebody else or nobody at all." —SYLVIA PLATH

- Every day should be spent focusing on developing what we believe to be our true gifts.
- When choosing who to work with (on projects or in business) opposing strengths can lead to the strongest partnerships.

CHAPTER 25

THREE BASIC TRUTHS ABOUT LEADERSHIP

As the saying goes, leadership is taken, not given. If you don't act like a leader and inspire people, no one will follow you. To use a *Star Wars* reference, as a leader, the Force is within you and you must find a way to use it to motivate and mobilize your team.

In the original *Star Wars*, Obi-Wan Kenobi told a young Luke Skywalker, "The Force is an energy field generated by all living things. It surrounds us, penetrates us and binds the galaxy together." In the *Star Wars* universe, those who master the use of the Force can harness and channel the very essence of life, which enables them to do extraordinary things. The Jedi use the Force to promote love, freedom and responsibility.

They do so with humility, courage and compassion, thus creating long-lasting bonds grounded in mutual learning and evolution.

Just like the Jedi, successful leaders understand that values and ethics play a much larger role in the success of a business than most people typically think. They also know that the way to establish personal credibility is by consistently living your core values and demonstrating that you are a leader people can trust.

Following are three basic truths that can help you become the leader you want to be:

1. You have to know your people.

The difference between being a manager and being a leader is that managers understand staff and leaders understand people. For managers, following the process is more important than anything else. Being efficient and knowing who has what skills, where they should be and what they should be doing trumps everything. Leaders understand their people: what motivates them, why they come to work each day, what's important outside of work and where they're heading in life. They also know what their people want and need from them.

More than almost anything else, people want leaders to listen. That doesn't mean leaders have to agree, but they do need to listen and try to understand. There are two different levels on which people want to be understood: intellectually and emotionally. At the intellectual level, they want the leader to understand what they are saying. At the emotional level, they want the leader to understand (or empathize with) what they are feeling, even if they don't agree.

Understanding your people as people, not employees, allows you to make more informed decisions that are tailored to the person, to frame your questions and requests in an effective way and to ultimately get the best out of your team. By getting to know his or her people, a good leader can make sure that the right people are focusing on the areas in which they'll be most effective – whilst keeping them engaged and motivated, encouraging them to think more broadly, and making sure they're always striving to achieve further success.

2. You need to adapt your leadership style for the person you are leading.

There is tremendous potential inside everyone and every member of the team has value. The challenge for you as a leader is in turning that potential into something meaningful. Great leadership is about your level of influence, not your level of authority. People follow the leader first and the vision second. If people aren't committed to you, they will not be committed to the vision you communicate. It's important to speak to people in their own language; part of building trust is knowing how to align what you want to accomplish with the wants and needs of those you are asking to do the work.

3. You must give your people something to believe in.

Great leaders create stability and drive change. Stability comes from building a strong foundation based on a commitment to shared values that give people meaning and a sense of identity beyond their role in the organization, and beyond the circumstances the organization or its people may be facing. We are drawn to leaders and organizations that are good at communicating what they believe and those who have the ability to make us feel like we belong and that together we can accomplish something great. Once you have captured the hearts and minds of people and built a

> "Leading is not the same as being the leader. Being the leader means you hold the highest rank, either by earning it, good fortune or navigating internal politics. Leading, however, means that others willingly follow you – not because they have to, not because they are paid to, but because they want to." —*SIMON SINEK*

stable foundation, you will find that they are no longer afraid of change, which is a necessary element for success in our fast-paced world.

CHAPTER 26

NOTHING TO LOSE

One of my favourite authors is John C. Maxwell.

It all began for him in June of 1969.

He was the pastor of a church in rural Indiana in a community called Hillman. With high hopes and boundless energy, he held his very first service – with three people in attendance. John Maxwell himself, his high school sweetheart Margaret (whom he later married) and one parishioner.

That was over 40 years ago.

Today, he has a worldwide audience in the millions and is considered the most influential leadership expert in the world.

He has written and published almost 100 books. I wish I could tell you that I have read them all but I haven't; I will say there are 60 John Maxwell books in my personal library. The ones I have read are all marked up with key thoughts and passages underlined in yellow marker. Each and every book is a feast of knowledge and wisdom.

One of John's favourite lines is, "Leadership is all about influence – the first person you need to influence is you."

How can we lead if we're not living the key leadership principles?

John's latest book, which for me has been the most inspiring, is titled *Intentional Living: Choosing a Life That Matters.*

It is almost 300 pages, and I read my copy in three days. It's a marvelous book. Towards the end of it, he talks about two mindsets: scarcity mindset and abundance mindset.

If you live with a scarcity mindset, you will get what you expect. You will have scarcity guaranteed.

If you live with an abundance mindset, at best you'll experience abundance. At worst, you'll get the scarcity you've already been experiencing; you have nothing to lose.

So take action – believe, anticipate, give and see what happens.

My fellow speaker Zig Ziglar once said:

"You can have everything in life you want, if you help enough people get what they want."

They all want abundance, so help them get it.

You cannot experience abundance while anticipating

scarcity. So why not try out a different mindset? Seek and share abundance.

CHAPTER 27

HOW A COUPLE OF SNAKE CHARMERS CHANGED MY CAREER PATH

Before I became a speaker, I tried my hand at standup comedy in England. Following a successful nine-week run on a BBC variety show, I hit the road as a headliner on a seven-week tour of big nightclubs in Birmingham, Leicester and Manchester.

The first week, I was booked at a nightclub in downtown Birmingham. Following the dress rehearsal with the orchestra and the MC, I asked the nightclub manager who else would be on the bill. He told me there would be a young female singer and then, pointing to an elderly couple in a dark corner, he said, "Those two people as well."

I asked what they did and he said, "They're snake charmers."

"Real snakes?" I asked incredulously.

"Yes, including pythons and lizards."

In my weirdest dreams, I hadn't imagined working with snake charmers and as I gazed across the room, I saw myself as a 60-year-old performer, having spent years on the road and still struggling to make a living in dimly lit clubs, the third act on the bill. All of a sudden, the light went on and I could see that this was not the business for me. At that precise moment, I could feel my dream of being a comic begin to die and I knew it was a major turning point in my life.

I didn't even wait to perform that night (an unpardonable sin in the business). Instead I rushed to a phone box and told my wife that I was quitting and coming home. Little did I know that my experiences on the comedy circuit were preparing me for my future on stage as a motivational speaker.

When you're headed in the wrong direction, it takes courage to put on the brakes and change course.

CHAPTER 28

GAME DAY PREP FOR SPEAKERS

J ust about every day, someone asks me about my speaking business. Usually, it's something related to how I prepare myself to give a talk.

My dear friend Jane Atkinson is a coach for both new and seasoned speakers; she helps them grow and improve their speaking business. Jane's newest book on the subject is titled *The Epic Keynote*, and she asked me to contribute some of my own tips, which I was happy to do.

Whether you're a speaker or simply give presentations in your workplace, these tips could be of use to you. So, let's assume you're contracted to speak at a hotel venue from 9:00 a.m. to 10:15 a.m. The audience is about 350 people. If I were in your shoes, my basic ritual would look like this.

First off, I want to know who's going to introduce me. Do they have my written introduction? What's their position within the organization, or are they in fact one of the sponsors?

Other than the introduction is there something else happening prior to my speech? For example, some kind of video from the association? Is the president of the organization providing some opening remarks? What's his or her name?

I'll also want to determine whether or not there's any leeway with my 75-minute address. What exactly is going to happen at 10:15 a.m. when I'm finished? Is there a coffee break? If so, how long? While most of these pre-speaking details might be in the contract, I find that in eight out of 10 presentations, the plan changes at the last minute, for all kinds of reasons, so it's good to stay on top of things.

When I arrive, I want to be sure to seek out the meeting planner or company organizer and introduce myself. Generally, an hour before the presentation, I do a sound check with the audio-visual people to ensure there is lighting on my face and find out how far I can wander from the podium while still keeping my face lit. I need to ensure that any equipment I'm using is compatible with the equipment they have, as sometimes this changes.

I'm also going to make sure I know what, if anything, has happened on the night before. For example, was there a party, reception, retirement or other celebration related to the company the night before that I can refer to in my opening remarks?

What to wear? Personally, I always sport a very smart suit that, if necessary, I have the hotel press the night before. I pair the suit with a white shirt, French cuffs, bold tie and very shiny shoes.

Now that I'm prepped, I have a few tried-and-true rituals to ensure my success. About 15 minutes prior to my expected introduction, I drink a glass of lukewarm water – cold water can restrict the pipes. I always say to myself, "I'm going to change the world today." (I know I'm not going to change the *whole* world, but I might change somebody's world.) I'm very fortunate that, while I've been in the business for over 35 years, the lead-up to each new speech fills me with the energy and excitement of my first time on stage.

Once I'm introduced, I walk with purpose onto the stage, no Cheshire grin. I always shake the hand of the introducer and gently lead them off the stage, recognizing that those two to three minutes are their time in the sun. I always keep eye contact with the introducer as I shake their hand as opposed to facing the audience.

Once the introducer has left and the audience starts to quiet, I can start. Sometimes I return to the podium and sometimes I begin my speech where I am, with as powerful an opening as I can.

Remember, the first words in a speech are very important.

They have to be engaging and you must have energy in your voice. You need to control the audience, but that doesn't mean yelling.

What's your backstage ritual?

CHAPTER 29

SAVE THE BEST FOR FIRST

The American comedian Louis C.K. has a unique approach for developing his standup act: "I take my closing bit and open with it. Because then I have to follow my strongest bit."

That's good advice for anyone who wants to take their performance to a higher level. If you're making a presentation to a client, start with your best ideas; if you're interviewing for a job, zero in on your biggest strengths and highlight them; if you're in a debate, open with your strongest argument.

By putting your best material out there first, you set high expectations on the part of your audience for the rest of your presentation and therefore challenge yourself to make sure everything that follows lives up to your strong opening. If the rest of your material doesn't measure up, you'll need to bump it up a couple notches and rework it until it does.

Honing your material takes time, practice and patience. Standup comedians spend years paying their dues on the circuit and figuring out what works with different audiences; so do speakers like myself.

If you're not sure about your material, try it out on a few people ahead of time and get their reaction, then rework and revise as necessary until you know it's the best it can be.

CHAPTER 30

10 WAYS TO MAKE
YOUR SPEECH BETTER

All leaders, sales professionals, content experts and ambitious professionals need to be good communicators. These 10 suggestions from Hall of Fame keynote speaker Patricia Fripp will be helpful when you deliver important presentations and want them to sound interesting.

1. People believe stories more readily than numbers or statistics. The hearer processes stories in three ways: intellectually, emotionally and visually (through visual aids and the speaker's movements). So start with a story and then use a statistic or visual to emphasize or elaborate the point.
2. Remember the "who" factor; audiences are people and

they are interested in other people. Use stories about people, particularly heroes. Look internally and externally in the company for the stories of your own everyday heroes.

3. Sound words build tension. Crack! (Was that lightning?) Build tension in the leadership message and then break it or relieve it as a means of holding audience attention. We all love suspense.

4. Smell and other sensory words also trigger the formation of memory. See, hear, smell, feel, taste . . . these all add texture and interest to your story.

5. Twist a phrase. "You can't teach a young dog old tricks." That's billionaire Warren Buffet, on why he consistently hires retirement-age managers rather than younger ones.

6. Add interest to your speaking with alliteration, repetition and rhythm.

7. Statistics should be used sparingly and distilled. Startling numbers are effective.

8. Quotes allow us to borrow the best that has been said or written. They can convey authority, brevity, relevance, humour, etc. Quotes put the human voice in your leadership message. Use contemporary quotes if possible. Be accurate. Use tone of voice to convey the quote, rather than saying "quote-unquote." Edit quotes down to the meat. Paraphrase quotes that are longer than one or two lines.

9. When discussing a big issue, "Tell the story of the war through the eyes of one soldier."

10. Remember, outside the privacy of your own home, all speaking is public speaking.

Patricia can be reached at:
415-753-6556
pfripp@fripp.com
www.fripp.com

CHAPTER 31

SPEAKING TIPS EVERY INTROVERT SHOULD KNOW

With approximately 22 million views, ethnographer Simon Sinek is the third-most-watched TED Talks presenter of all time, not to mention a bestselling author. He's also a self-confessed introvert. Pretty ironic, wouldn't you say? How did Sinek learn to give such awesome presentations? If you ask him, he did it by facing his biggest fears head on. He also realized that becoming a great speaker who inspires others doesn't just happen because you wish for it; he's spent years studying others and tirelessly practicing his craft.

Here are seven tips for delivering speeches that Simon shared with *Entrepreneur* magazine.

1. Don't talk right away.

"A lot of people start talking right away and it's out of nerves," Sinek says. "That communicates a little bit of insecurity and fear." Instead, quietly walk out on stage. Then take a deep breath, find your place, wait a few seconds and begin. "I know it sounds long and tedious and it feels excruciatingly awkward when you do it, but it shows the audience you're totally confident and in charge of the situation."

2. Show up to give, not to take.

If you're just there to sell your book, get people to follow you on social media or flog your latest produce or idea, it's not going to go well for you. "We are highly social animals," says Sinek. "People can tell if you're a giver or a taker and people are more likely to trust a giver, a speaker that gives them value, teaches them something new and inspires them."

3. Make eye contact with audience members one by one.

Constantly scanning the audience doesn't help you connect. It's much more effective to at make eye contact with specific audience members throughout your speech. Each time you finish a sentence, find a new person to connect with so it's like you're having a conversation with your audience and not speaking at them, but with them.

4. Speak as slowly as you can.

Nervousness can make your words speed up without you really noticing, but your audience will. Sometimes you just have to go quiet for a moment and take a long, deep breath.

Don't worry, the audience will wait for you. According to Sinek, it's practically impossible to speak too slowly on stage. "It's incredible that you can stand on stage and speak so slowly that there are several seconds between each of your words and people . . . will . . . hang . . . on . . . your . . . every . . . word."

5. Ignore the naysayers.

Not everyone will like you, but it's OK to ignore the ones who don't. Instead, focus on your supporters – they're the ones who are visibly engaged and nodding yes. If you give your attention to the audience members who are interacting with you in a positive way, you'll be much more confident and relaxed and your whole presentation will go much better.

6. Turn your nerves into excitement.

Sinek shares that he learned this trick from watching the Olympics, where he noticed when reporters asked Olympic athletes the question, "Were you nervous?" Their inevitable answer was, "No, I was excited." These competitors were reinterpreting the body's signs of nervousness, such as a pounding heart and tense nerves, as side effects of excitement and exhilaration. Sinek's advice: When you're up on stage and you feel those nerves, say to yourself out loud, "I'm not nervous, I'm excited!"

7. Say thank you when you're done.

Applause is a gift, and when you receive a gift, it's only right to express your thanks. Sinek always closes his presentations with the simple yet powerful words: "Thank you."

CHAPTER 32

MEETING JOHN MAXWELL

A s I've alluded to, I've been a fan and admirer of John C. Maxwell for many years. He is considered the foremost leadership expert in the world.

Having the opportunity to meet him had eluded me until January 2 of this year, when I was invited to a private session with him at the Hotel Vancouver, courtesy of Jeff Williams, the President of Absolute Results Productions Ltd.

About 40 business leaders attended to meet him personally and get a photo together as well as a signed copy of his latest book, *Living Intentionally*. The meet-and-greet was followed by a 60-minute fireside chat with a Q&A session.

It was an opportunity I could not pass up.

As the hour approached and I entered the room, I decided

to pay strict attention to his every move and see how he interacted with all the guests.

When John entered the room, he was shorter than I expected, wearing a sport jacket and slacks and a pink open-necked shirt. I watched as he was introduced and greeted the guests. With each person, he offered a smile, looked them in the eye and inquired about their career or where they lived in Vancouver. It was a three-to-five minute encounter.

I was about the fifth person he was introduced to and received the same warm and friendly greeting.

As he was about to move onto the next person, I put my arm on his shoulder and said, "John, I know you have written about 100 books. I haven't read them all, but I have purchased and read 61 of your books from cover to cover." He said, "Thank you . . . that makes both you and my mother." We both laughed.

He then turned to the next person waiting beside him and, pointing to me, said, "Peter has written and published 19 books."

What an amazing connection!

The next morning I told my assistant Heidi Christie this story and she reminded me that about a month before this event, she was asked to send John Maxwell my entire CV, so he must have read it, and the fact that I had written and published 19 books stood out.

The important part of this interaction is he read the

CV, connected it to me and remembered this one fact. Very impressive.

As a renowned leadership expert and famous author, John Maxwell could have simply come to this event, shook hands, said hello and everyone would have left happy. By doing more and engaging in a personal way, he made a lasting impression.

Here's a little more wisdom from John Maxwell:

"The best leaders are readers of people. They have the intuitive ability to understand others by discerning how they feel and recognizing what they sense."

"Remember, man does not live on bread alone: sometimes he needs a little buttering up."

> "There is one longing almost as deep and imperious as the desire for food and sleep. It is the desire to be great. It is the desire to be important."
> — *DALE CARNEGIE*

CHAPTER 33

HOW GOOD IS YOUR INFORMATION?

"There's no Nobel Prize for fact-checking." —John Oliver

One thing I like about comedians, and this is probably what attracted me to the comedy circuit as a young man, is that they hold up a mirror and reflect back how ridiculous, naïve and contradictory we humans can sometimes be. This is particularly true of satirists like Stephen Colbert and John Oliver, both of whom use hysterical rants and outrageous commentary to encourage their audiences to think critically about what is happening in the world around them.

In a recent episode of his popular HBO show *Last Week Tonight*, Oliver reeled off headlines from a number of "scientific" studies as examples. "Hugging your dog is bad for your dog," read one. "Drinking a glass of red wine is just as good as spending an hour at the gym," said another. Oliver's rant was about how too often, we don't question the validity of the information that is being fed to us, and worse yet, we pass it on to others as fact.

Turns out, the study about dog hugging came from a psychology professor at the University of British Columbia who looked at a random selection of 250 photos on Google and Flickr of people hugging dogs and determined that, in four out of five cases, the dogs exhibited at least one sign of stress. So even though there was no actual scientific study conducted and no subjects (dogs or humans) were observed in person, this story was published in the magazine *Psychology Today* and widely shared by reputable media outlets around the world, including the *New York Times*.

I think it's human nature to want to believe the things that we see and hear, especially when they come from a source that we trust and respect. Who doesn't want to hear on the news that a new scientific study shows not only is coffee not bad for us, but it prevents cancer and makes us younger by 10 years? How likely are we to question information that validates something we enjoy doing? In my experience, not very likely. But that leaves us relying on others to vet our information, which can have serious consequences.

Consider this: an asteroid is hurtling toward Earth and people are relying on scientists to blast it to smithereens in order to save the planet and all of humanity. If even one of those NASA scientists botches the calculations for their part in destroying the asteroid and it crashes into Earth because they didn't check their data, then faulty information really was responsible, wasn't it?

I know that may sound ridiculous, but put it in the context of your own business; if you're making important decisions about your markets, your customers, your competitors or your industry based on information that you haven't bothered to verify, you're putting your business – and your livelihood – at risk.

Think about how much information you come into contact with on a daily basis – clearly an insane amount. How much of it is accurate? How much is blatantly wrong? Do you go out of your way to verify or validate information before sending it on? How does inaccurate information affect your life and the lives of those around you? Perfect information isn't the goal, but getting quality information is not that much of a stretch. Think about the information-packed world we live in and find ways to improve the info you use and pass on to others.

Here are some questions to ask that will help you verify your information:

- Who is the real source and are they reputable?
- What was their purpose in collecting this information? Does it relate to what you will use it for? Did they have a bias you should be aware of? Were they sponsored?
- When was the information collected? Timeliness is one of the most important elements with information. Is your info current or have there been significant developments in the interim that would make it unreliable?
- How was the information collected? From the Internet, through interviews, focus groups, case studies, database searches, etc.

> "The problem with the Internet is that it gives you everything – reliable material and crazy material.
> So the problem becomes, how do you discriminate?"
> —*UMBERTO ECO*

- Has the information been verified by a reliable third party?
- What information was collected? Is this everything? Is there context for how you will use it? Are there relevant missing elements that could invalidate the information for your intended use?
- Does the information relate to what you already know?

CHAPTER 34

10 PRODUCTIVITY HACKS THAT ACTUALLY WORK

We could all be a little more productive in our day-to-day lives. Productivity starts with a determination to change. Perhaps some of these tricks, shared by entrepreneur and speaker Murray Newlands, might encourage renewed efficiency in your daily routine:

Procrastination, frankly, just feels good . . . right up to the minute when we recall that we really must get things done. That's when it gets ugly. All of us hop into ninja mode and scramble around until everything gets accomplished – of course, half-heartedly. Then we vow to ourselves that we'll never procrastinate again. But, deep inside, all of us know it'll happen repeatedly. It's a vicious pattern and it won't stop unless we break it . . . by becoming productive. Here are 10 productivity tricks successful people use.

1. Wake up earlier.

If you rise one hour earlier than usual each day, you will be shocked at how much you will get accomplished in a week. Additionally, rising at the same time each day stabilizes your circadian rhythm. Having a circadian rhythm that is steady allows you to become more productive during the daytime because you will be more alert and energetic.

2. Create a list.

Few things are more satisfying than crossing an activity off the to-do list. It is tangible evidence that you truly got something accomplished and it may motivate you to tackle your whole list in a day.

3. Take baby steps.

Did you ever put a task off only to find out, when you finally got around to it, that it took just 10 minutes to do? A task, oftentimes, seems more daunting than it really is.

4. Eat your broccoli first.

If you don't like something but you know it's good for you or needs to be done, do it (or eat it) first. Then you can relax and enjoy everything else. For example, if you do the most difficult task first thing in the morning, you'll alleviate yourself of stress and better appreciate the remainder of your day.

5. Beat the clock.

You can play a game: Try to beat the clock! Set a timer for 50 minutes and accomplish a task with complete concentration. When that time is up, take a 10-minute break. Then reset your timer and start working again for 50 minutes; then take a 10-minute break. Repeat this cycle until everything is completed.

6. Voice commitments.

A promise to yourself is a lot easier to break than one you've given to somebody else. You are more likely to get something accomplished if you know someone else is going to hold you accountable. Locate an entrepreneurial buddy to monitor your progress as you start a business.

7. Remove all temptations.

Checking your Facebook alerts and reading a text might seem like a harmless action that takes no more than five seconds, but doing this really snaps you out of your zone of concentration (plus, it takes time to get back in the zone). Not just that, doing it repeatedly throughout the day really adds up to a lot of time wasted.

8. Enforce the five-minute rule.

If an activity takes five minutes or less to finish, do it immediately. This rule is particularly great for responding to emails or tidying up a room. When faced with an activity, instantly ask yourself if it will take five minutes or less to accomplish. If so, do it!

9. Trap yourself.

If all else fails, it's time to leave yourself without any option. This means taking drastic measures to make yourself finish a task. For instance, if you have to change your car's oil, have somebody lock you out of your home until your car's oil pan is put away and clean.

10. Accept that you're just human like everyone else.

Know that nobody is perfect and you will not be rejected for not flawlessly performing a task. As faced with a challenging activity, tell yourself, "I am only human, and it is all right to make a mistake."

CHAPTER 35

DRIFTING

How different is a leaf floating on top of a stream from a fish actively swimming in the centre of that stream? At first the leaf swirls in the light, but as it drifts further from the centre and the current slows, it gets snagged on twigs and debris at the edge. In contrast, the fish chooses again and again to stay in the flow, gaining strength and momentum from the invigorating current.

Several years ago now, Gretchen Rubin, author of *The Happiness Project*, posted a quiz on her blog about "drifting," which is exactly what the name suggests – letting ourselves be carried away by circumstances rather than taking control of, and responsibility for, what is happening in our lives. But don't be mistaken: drifting isn't about doing nothing. In fact, most people work very hard when they're drifting, often because they are trying to avoid facing up to the fact that they're doing what they think they should or what someone else wants them to, rather than what they truly want to do.

Here are a few excerpts from Rubin's quiz. As the author explains, "The more checks you make, the greater your risk of being adrift."

☐ *I often have the peculiar feeling that I'm living someone else's life, or that this isn't my "real" life.*

☐ *I complain about my situation but I don't spend much time trying to figure out ways to make it better.*

☐ *I spend a lot of time daydreaming about a completely different life as an escape from what I'm doing now.*

☐ *There is something in my life that I used to be passionate about, but now I never allow myself to indulge in it.*

To take the full quiz, visit *gretchenrubin.com / happiness_ project / 2011 / 02 / back-by-popular-demand-quz-are-you-drifting*.

We aren't here for long, so it doesn't make sense to allow ourselves to drift away on the current or get caught up in someone else's idea of who we should be. We need to make the most of every moment. Make a commitment to yourself to stay in the flow.

CHAPTER 36

YOU CAN *GET* ANYONE IF YOU TRY

W e all have people we don't *get*. Everyone's different and sometimes it's hard to understand those people we perceive to be *very* different from us. It can also be difficult to open up and accept people we don't feel comfortable around, but the reality is: we don't always get to choose who spends time around us, whether it's a colleague at work, a client or an in-law who's suddenly part of our family. So it makes sense to at least try to understand where others are coming from.

According to Dave Kerpen, author of *The Art of People: 11 Simple People Skills That Will Get You Everything You Want,* the first step is to reach out to the person and get to know something about them. "Be interested, rather than interesting," advises Kerpen. "Let them talk about what's important to them."

It's not necessary to like everyone whom you interact with, but by getting to know a little more about them, at least you can have some empathy or understanding of who they are, which will help you develop a more productive and beneficial relationship. If you have to, consider it an experiment to see if it's possible for you to learn to understand someone very different from you. So go ahead and ask them out for coffee.

Once you're face to face, keep these tips in mind:

- Most of what people think or do isn't about you, it's about them. People don't care about *you*. This isn't because they are mean or hurtful, but simply because they are mostly focused on themselves and their concerns, so don't be offended.
- If you haven't been up front about what you want, need, or how you feel, don't get angry when others aren't responding to you the way you want them to. This goes for work relationships as well as personal ones.
- Look for things you have in common rather than differences. People are more likely to remember your similarities and feel a bond when you have the same interests.
- People are more likely to help you if there's something in

it for them. There are basically four different things that motivate us as humans to help others:

1. *Transactions* – If I buy a car from you, both of us benefit. I get a vehicle, which I want. You get money to improve your lifestyle. This is the predominant form of "selfish altruism" between people who don't have emotional bonds.

2. *Familial* – Blood is thicker than water. We are designed to protect people who share our genes. This sometimes also includes extremely close friends and other loved ones.

3. *Philanthropy* – Helping someone is a sign of status and power. Many species of primates offer assistance as a sign of dominance. People act similarly, offering help to boost their reputation as well as self-esteem. That's what charity is all about.

4. *You owe me one* – Many relationships are based on the idea that if I help you, one day you will help me in return; it's called implied reciprocity.

- Finally, remember relationships are a shared responsibility. Don't wait to be invited to gatherings or for others to approach you. Reach out to them and show that you're interested and approachable.

Now for your homework: Write down the names of three people in your life with whom you're struggling to connect.

Commit to asking one of them to have coffee with you in the next week, then walk into the coffee meeting determined to *get* this person – even though you might find that you still don't like them.

CHAPTER 37

LET YOURSELF (AND OTHERS) MAKE MISTAKES

Social psychologist Heidi Grant Halvorson has an interesting take on mistakes. According to her research, people who give themselves "permission to screw up," actually make fewer mistakes and master new skills faster. The reason for this is that they take a "get better" approach to goals rather than a "be good" approach.

Here's how it works: When we have a be-good mindset, we put a lot of pressure on ourselves to perform well; this can create a lot of anxiety, particularly when it is a task that we haven't performed many times before. Nothing interferes with performance quite like anxiety and that makes us much more prone to mistakes and, ultimately, failure.

However, when we tackle a goal with a get-better approach, our focus turns away from our performance to learning and improving. As a result, we accept that it is fine to make some mistakes along the way, which allows us to stay motivated and focused on our goal despite any setbacks that may occur.

Halvorson, who is the author of *Succeed: How We Can Reach Our Goals*, offers three helpful steps for reframing goals:

1. Start by embracing the fact that when something is difficult and unfamiliar, it will take time to really get a handle on it. You might make some mistakes and that's OK.

2. Remember to ask for help when you run into trouble. Needing help doesn't mean you aren't capable – in fact, the opposite is true. Only the very foolish believe they can do everything on their own.

3. Don't compare yourself to others. Instead, compare your performance today to your performance yesterday; getting better is about progress, not perfection.

When you give yourself permission to make mistakes, your focus shifts from you to your goal, which is where it should be. Something else I learned from my mentor Joe Segal: don't get caught up in trying to achieve perfection. "Ultimately, it is persistence that will pay off, so forget about perfection," says Joe. "There really isn't enough time in the world for us to worry about getting it right all the time. Besides, perfection isn't about doing a good job, it is about being in control and it feeds an overbearing need to be right. It is a far better thing to be persistent; find a goal that captures your imagination and strive to achieve it."

As a leader, it is important to let the people you are leading know that it's OK for them to make mistakes as well. By modelling and coaching this behaviour, you give others within your organization permission to make mistakes and grow.

CHAPTER 38

JUST BREATHE

Holding onto anything, according to Deepak Chopra, whether it is an event in the past or a preconceived idea of what the future should be, is like holding your breath. Ultimately, you'll suffocate. Letting go of things and learning to live in the present moment can be extremely difficult (I know it is for me), but "mindfulness practice," as it is often called, can be as simple as breathing. Seriously, one of the simplest ways to experience living in the moment can be done as you go about your daily activities, and it's all about focusing on your breathing.

Here's an exercise to try. It involves breathing from your belly, not your chest.

First, sit or stand in a relaxed position. Now slowly inhale through your nose until you feel that you can't take in any more air. As you prepare to slowly exhale, firm up your belly and tighten your abdominal muscles to push the air up and out of your lungs. Repeat this process several times. That's it!

Here are a few more tips:

1. As you breathe, let your abdomen expand outward rather than raising your shoulders. This is a more relaxed and natural way to breathe. It also helps your lungs fill more fully with fresh air and push out more old air.

2. Try a few breaths any time you want to release tension or for several minutes as a form of meditation.

3. If you like, you can make your throat a little tighter as you exhale so the air comes out like an exaggerated sigh. This type of breathing is used in yoga and can yield additional relaxation.

Mindfulness is an acquired skill. Its stress-reduction benefits are well documented and there are many positive emotional and spiritual side effects as well. And it has a bonus: as your skill increases, you will, by definition, let go of things from the past or worries about the future.

Take some time to practice mindfulness and consciously breathe every day.

CHAPTER 39

PEOPLE BEFORE POLICIES

U.S. retail giant Nordstrom opened a store in Vancouver in early 2015. They have legendary customer service.

Nordstrom places emphasis on people, not policies. And so every employee receives the following instructions when they begin working for the company:

WELCOME TO NORDSTROM

We're glad to have you with our company.

Our No. 1 goal is to provide outstanding customer service.

Set both your personal and professional goals high.

We have great confidence in your ability to achieve them.

NORDSTROM RULES:

Rule #1: Use your good judgment in all situations.

There will be no additional rules. Please feel free to ask your department manager, store manager or divisional manager any questions at any time.

CHAPTER 40

IN PRAISE OF OCKHAM'S RAZOR

We live in a complicated world and as a result we often get overwhelmed with details and forget that there is genius in keeping things as simple as possible.

William of Ockham was a British-born medieval philosopher who practiced a method of problem solving based on the law of parsimony that has become known as "Ockham's Razor."

Ockham said, "The simplest and most direct resolution is usually the best solution to any problem. More complicated remedies should only be applied when the existence of a simpler solution has been ruled out."

As humans, we often make the mistake of overcomplicating both our problems and our goals. What Ockham realized is that the more complicated something is (even if it is a good idea), the less likely it is to ever be implemented. Therefore, if you have a problem and are torn between two different solutions that in all likelihood will be equally effective, by applying Ockham's razor, you should choose the solution that is less complicated.

Ockham also said, "Plurality should not be posited without necessity." Many of you will know this more commonly as the KISS principle, an acronym for "Keep It Simple, Stupid."

The acronym was first coined by Kelly Johnson, a lead engineer with Lockheed who worked on the Lockheed U-2 and SR-71 Blackbird spy planes, among other aircraft.

As the story goes, Johnson once handed a team of design engineers a handful of tools with the challenge that the jet aircraft they were designing must be repairable by an average mechanic in the field under combat conditions using only those tools. Hence, the "stupid" refers to the relationship between the way things break and the resources available to fix them.

Challenge yourself to "Keep It Simple" when choosing how you will solve problems or achieve your goals.

CHAPTER 41

GOOD ADVICE NEVER GOES OUT OF STYLE

Several years ago I was presented with the chance to be chair of the Vancouver Board of Trade (now known as the Greater Vancouver Board of Trade). I thought it was a position over my head, but obviously others didn't. I was encouraged by Board of Trade managing director Darcy Rezac, my predecessor Carole Taylor and Board member Graham Stamp, as well as past chairs Brandt Louie, Rick Turner and Allan Skidmore.

That's a pretty nice squad to have cheering for you, so I took motivational speaker Les Brown's advice: "Jump and the net will appear."

I jumped, and it was such a good decision. I learned

so much in that year and spoke at hundreds of events, including a very special dinner hosted by Joe and Rosalie Segal for former United States Ambassador to Canada, Paul Cellucci. I even had the opportunity to represent the Board of Trade at the annual Davos Summit in Switzerland. It was like getting a PhD in only one year!

I recently purchased a book by George H. Knox titled *Thoughts That Inspire*, published in 1905. It contains great advice on how to succeed after you've made your great leap. On pages 43 and 44, Knox, president of the London Chamber of Commerce, wrote:

- *Have a definite aim.*
- *Go straight to it.*
- *Master all details.*
- *Always know more than you are expected to know.*
- *Treat failures as stepping stones to further effort.*
- *At times be bold; and always be prudent.*
- *Make good use of other men's brains.*
- *Listen well; answer cautiously; decide promptly.*
- *The majority in the end are beaten by the minority.*
- *Remember that difficulties are only made to be overcome.*
- *Never put your hand out further than you can draw back.* (I love that one.)
- *Preserve, by all means in your power, a sound mind and a sound body.*

Volume one of *Thoughts That Inspire* was published in 1905, followed by Volume two in 1909 – they would both make great additions to your library. You can order them through AbeBooks.

CHAPTER 42

GOODBYE, DAL RICHARDS
(1918-2015)

It was about 19 minutes to midnight on New Year's Eve, 2015. Surrounded by his wife Muriel and other family members, Dal Richards peacefully slipped away from this life to the next. Had he lived another 19 minutes, he would have entered his 98th year. That's something.

They called him the King of Swing. He was one of the last big band leaders – a true Canadian and a Vancouver icon. Just about everyone in B.C. knows about Dal Richards. He was recognized literally everywhere he went and he was admired, respected, revered and much loved by people of all ages.

I first met Dal some 40 years ago when I was on the Variety Telethon, which was broadcast on BCTV, live from the

Queen Elizabeth Theatre in downtown Vancouver. The Dal Richards Orchestra was a featured part of the 24-hour show which raised money for kids with special needs. Even back then, his presence commanded attention.

Over the years, we became more than acquaintances – I liked him and I think he liked me. We were both in show business – he a musician and big band leader, and me a comic, MC and professional speaker. Dal called every show a "gig"! We often compared how many gigs we did a year – I could never keep pace with him.

Here are a couple of stories you might not know about Dal and a few lessons that he taught me.

1. When he was presented with the nation's highest honour, The Order of Canada, Dal said to me, "When I return from Ottawa, let's have coffee and I'll tell you about this experience." Upon his return, good to his word, he called and we went to the Vancouver Club for lunch. He showed me his Order of Canada medal and told me how impressive and humbling the entire experience was.

Here was a saxophone player among so many other deserving Canadians receiving our country's highest distinction . . . and to think, it almost never happened. Here's why:

One morning, a few months before the ceremony, Dal was at home in his pajamas and dressing gown having breakfast when the doorbell rang. It was a registered letter from the Government of Canada. He thought it might be a bill for past taxes owed to the Canada Revenue Agency, so he put the unopened letter down and finished his breakfast. "A registered letter, indeed, asking for more money," he mumbled to himself. A few hours later he grudgingly decided to open it and see what they wanted. He was stunned! The letter was asking him if he would accept the Order of Canada.

Lesson learned: Don't jump to conclusions (even when it's a letter from the government).

2. Dal was once performing at a sold-out Orpheum Theatre, which holds about 2,800 people. Following his show, he asked the general manager, Ivan Ackers, how he did. Ivan told him, "You never once looked at the balcony. Fifty per cent of the audience was there and you didn't look up, not once."

Lesson learned: Never forget the balcony of your life; no matter what profession you're in, everyone likes to be acknowledged.

3. I had the privilege of being on the board of directors of the Pacific National Exposition for six years.

Dal performed at the PNE for 75 years. Following his last performance each year, he always asked the PNE president, Mike McDaniel, "How about next year's contract?"

Mike told him, "Dal, you don't need a contract. If you want to play at the PNE next year, just let me know and you're on!"

But Dal still asked.

Lesson learned: Don't take anything for granted, you have to earn it.

I believe that Dal is in a better place these days and conducting the biggest orchestra with his largest audience ever!

Bless you, my friend. Rest in peace.

CHAPTER 43

LEAD LIKE A MARINE

The U.S. Marines have 14 leadership traits that they teach to all personnel, regardless of their role. The reasoning behind this is to ensure every individual in the organization is prepared to lead when called upon. What I find interesting is the understanding that not all of these traits are instinctive and neither is leadership for many, but it can be taught.

These are the 14 traits:

1. Courage
2. Decisiveness
3. Dependability
4. Endurance

5. Enthusiasm

6. Initiative

7. Integrity

8. Judgment

9. Justice

10. Knowledge

11. Loyalty

12. Tact

13. Unselfishness

14. Usefulness

Practice developing all of these traits and you will be a role model and a leader who others want to follow.

CHAPTER 44

DON'T BACK DOWN FROM THE SHARKS

S tand your ground! Navy SEALs are taught to survive encounters in shark-infested waters by exhibiting no fear and using a "punch in the snout" if necessary. "There are lots of 'sharks' in the world," says Admiral William H. McRaven, a former SEAL team commander and director of U.S. Joint Special Operations Command, "but if you want to change the world, don't back down from the sharks!"

Compromising your values to go along with something you don't agree with or believe in has a negative impact on your mental and emotional well-being. It also allows others to take advantage of you, which, in and of itself, is bound to make you feel angry and resentful.

Here are four things to remember when confronted with difficult situations or people:

1.   Silence is agreement.

The longer you stay quiet, the harder it is to speak, and if you don't stand up for yourself, who will? If you don't agree with what is happening and you say nothing, others may consider the issue as much your fault as the person who caused the problem. In the long run, staying silent destroys trust and creates bad blood.

2.   Do it for the greater good.

Not asserting yourself because you don't want to offend never really helps. When things are headed in the wrong direction or the situation has been taken over by someone with a forceful, bullying nature, it's selfish to put your own desire to avoid discomfort above the needs of your team. The worst that will happen when you speak up is that someone may challenge your perspective, but at least the issue will be out in the open. And who knows – you may give someone else the courage to speak up as well.

> "The world is not always the most pleasant place. Eventually your parents leave you and nobody is going to go out of their way to protect you unconditionally. You need to learn to stand up for yourself and what you believe."
> —ANONYMOUS

3. You may not be the only one who sees it that way.

If you never share your ideas, no one will know you have them – and they won't be in a position to support those ideas or go to bat for you when it matters. Sharing your perspective gives others the opportunity to show their support.

4. No one pays attention to a wallflower.

People don't automatically recognize your skills, values, ambitions and needs when you are quiet. If you wait around for people to ask you what you'd like or read your mind, you will likely end up with projects you don't want, miss out on promotions you do want or have to accept tasks you don't have the time or skills to complete.

CHAPTER 45

HOW'S YOUR GAME?

As my wife and I head out onto the green in sunny Palm Springs, a story I included in my very first book, *How to Soar With the Eagles*, comes to mind.

It took me a long time to get the hang of golf. For years, golfing friends and colleagues would tell me, "There's nothing more relaxing than a game of golf."

And I would tell them in response, "There's nothing more frustrating, intimidating and demeaning."

For many, golf relieves stress. That satisfying click as the club connects and the ball flies off into the stratosphere; to see the ball leap from the sand and bite the green six inches from the pin; to putt and watch the ball roll with seeming confidence to a rattling end in the cup – all very satisfying moments . . . unless you don't know how to make those moments happen. In which case, golf can be a hapless misadventure filled with hooks, slices, whiffs, chops, flying divots, sand in your shoes and atrocious language.

Red Poling, former CEO and chairman of the Ford Motor Company and an accomplished golfer, often said that his office game parallelled his golf game. According to Red, the three most important things in business and in golf are consistency, dependability and predictability.

"If my game is good, it's because I'm consistent in my swing. I don't need a big, wide fairway," explains Red, who believes in practicing fundamentals and focusing on whatever is going to win you the game. "Everyone likes to hit a drive the farthest, but you actually use a driver less than a putter."

Finally, he stresses the importance of giving full attention to the task at hand. "As you walk up to the next shot, you're not taking a stroll to check out the beautiful scenery around you. You're watching the terrain, noticing the impact of the wind, surveying the green, checking the hazards and planning your next shot."

Next time, whether you're on the green or in the office, ask yourself how consistent, dependable and predictable your game is.

CHAPTER 46

YOU DO THE MATH

"The richest people in the world look for and build networks.
Everyone else looks for work." —Robert Kiyosaki

Self-improvement guru Dale Carnegie said, "You can make more friends in two months by becoming interested in other people than you can in two years by trying to get other people interested in you."

The average number of people at a wedding is about 250. The average number of people at a funeral is about 250. Most people have at least 250 connections through social media. A box of business cards holds about 250 cards. So when you get right down to it, most people know 250 other people, give or take.

That means every time you make a good impression or cultivate a relationship with one person, you have actually expanded your influence by 250 people. If you consider that this applies to every single person you meet, the multiplier effect for increasing your network is exponential.

Think about that the next time you find yourself sitting or standing next to a stranger with a few minutes to spare (whether

> "Networking is marketing. Marketing yourself, marketing your uniqueness, marketing what you stand for."
> —*CHRISTINE COMAFORD-LYNCH*

it's in a business setting, at your child's soccer practice, standing in line at the supermarket or at a social function). Rather than checking email on your phone or staring at the wall in uncomfortable silence, strike up a conversation and get to know the person next to you. You never know who they might know or when they might need what you have to offer (people like to do business with people who are friendly and engaging).

And if you can't think of anything else to talk about, why not open with a comment about how that *BCBusiness* guy Peter Legge says that everyone knows about 250 people.

CHAPTER 47

TAKE A NAP, IT'S GOOD FOR YOU

A feature story in *Chatelaine*'s March 2016 issue caught my attention. Its heading was "Doze Your Way To Success."

Studies have shown that people who take a daily nap have lower blood pressure and increased tolerance for frustration.

Kimberly Cote, a psychology professor and director of Brock University's sleep research lab, says napping is proven to boost alertness, mood and memory. There are other benefits as well; research conducted by the European Society of Cardiology found that people who took a daily nap had lower blood pressure, and the University of Michigan linked napping at work to increased tolerance for frustration, higher productivity and less impulsive behaviour.

Dr. Cote recommends taking a 20-minute power nap in the afternoon when you can, which is just long enough to get the benefits of rest without drifting into the deep stages of sleep.

Some people might equate napping with being lazy, but being lazy isn't necessarily bad, according to Bill Gates, who says, "I choose a lazy person to do a hard job, because a lazy person will find an easy way to do it."

Although he didn't like to talk about it, the prolific inventor Thomas Edison was a habitual napper, which was probably the secret to his remarkable productivity. Once, when Henry Ford dropped by Edison's lab for a visit, Edison's assistant stopped him from entering the office because Edison was napping. When Ford looked confused and said, "But I thought Edison didn't sleep very much," the assistant replied, "He doesn't sleep very much at all, he just naps a lot."

A form of micro napping practiced by the likes of Salvador Dali, Einstein and Aristotle has more recently gained scientific credence for its usefulness in sparking creative ideas and problem solving. Known as a hypnogogic nap, the way Dali did it was to fall asleep sitting in a chair with a key in his hand and a pie plate on the floor directly below the hand with the key. As he dozed off, his hand would relax. When his hand relaxed enough to drop the key, the clank of the key on the pie plate would wake him up and he would immediately jump to his canvas to paint based on the ideas that came to him in that hypnogogic state between dreaming and wakefulness. Einstein described using a similar technique to sharpen his problem-solving abilities during the day. The trick with micro napping is to wake yourself before you get to stage 2 sleep, after which it is much harder to regain full alertness.

CHAPTER 48

THE LAST FIVE MINUTES

We all have days when things don't go as we planned – that's life. But when it happens on a regular basis, it's probably time to re-evaluate daily habits and routines.

In his blog for the *Harvard Business Review*, Peter Bregman, author of *Point B: A Short Guide to Leading a Big Change*, explains that there's a simple reason why we often don't realize when things start to go offside. "We rarely take the time to pause, breathe and think about what's working and what's not. There's just too much to do and no time to reflect."

Bregman suggests that we all set aside the last five minutes of each day to review what took place.

"Look at your calendar and compare what actually happened – the meetings you attended, the work you got done, the conversations you had, the people with whom you interacted – with what you wanted to happen," suggests Bregman. "Then ask yourself three sets of questions:

How did the day go? What success did I experience? What challenges did I encounter?

What did I learn today? About myself? About others? What do I plan to do differently, or the same, tomorrow?

Who did I interact with? Anyone I need to update, thank, ask a question, share feedback?"

According to Bregman, the last set of questions is invaluable in terms of maintaining and growing relationships.

"If we don't pause to think about it, we're apt to overlook these kinds of communications," he says. "And we often do. But in a world where we depend on others to achieve anything in life, they are essential."

Give yourself time to reflect every day. Put it in your calendar; it's only five minutes but it's time well spent.

CHAPTER 49

JUST BE YOURSELF

Like many of us, former Tsawwassen First Nation Chief Kim Baird sought out the advice of mentors when she was a young woman embarking on her career, but some of the advice she received didn't fit with her own values and that created a problem.

"Earlier in my career, I actually had a mentor tell me I was naïve because of my approach, because I wasn't pounding the table with my fist," she says. "It really undermined my confidence for a period of time. I had to learn the hard way that I could be effective just being myself, and since then I've been successful by following my own style of leadership. Ultimately the best advice is something I've heard many places, which is to be yourself. Now they have a fancy word for it: authenticity. It just means that you can be effective without having to have a persona. I've found that, as a woman, I have a very collaborative style, which is not seen as typical [for] chiefs and negotiators."

As a chief, one of Baird's biggest dreams was to sign and implement British Columbia's first urban land treaty (Tsawwassen is located within the Metro Vancouver region). As chief from 1999 to 2012, Baird represented her people throughout the negotiation process that ended in April 2009 with a treaty giving the Tsawwassen Nation full autonomy. By staying true to herself and her own dream, Baird accomplished something that many people believed impossible, and she continues to pursue her dreams – doing it on her own terms, based on her own values. In recognition of her exemplary leadership and vision, she was named to the Order of Canada in 2014.

PART 3

THE STRENGTH OF CHARACTER

Seest thou a person diligent in their business?
They shall stand before Kings.
—Proverbs 22:29

CHAPTER 50

WHO ARE YOU?

I t's a powerful question.

A speaker friend of mine from Seattle tells a story about crossing the border between Washington and British Columbia. When he got to the customs agent, he was asked:

- Who are you?
- Where are you going?
- What do you have to declare?

These questions work well at the border because the answers can reveal so much.

They also work for life.

So, who are you? Are you a person of character?

In a presentation he gave to students at Vancouver's John Oliver High School (from which he graduated in 1947), iconic Vancouver billionaire Jimmy Pattison (a man whom, it should be clear by now, I hold in the highest regard as a person of impeccable character), told the students they can achieve their dreams if they work hard, tell the truth and never fear failure.

"We all fail," he said in his presentation. "I have failed so many times but it never discourages me, I just pick up and keep going." Jimmy said he wanted to share with the students some of the obstacles he had overcome to become the president and CEO of the Jim Pattison Group, which has interests in cars, grocery stores, advertising and other sectors.

He also shared how his family ended up living in a rented house on East 44th after having to move from a home on 33rd Avenue because the landlord raised the rent from $2.50 per month to $27.50 and his father couldn't afford the new price – his was by no means a privileged childhood.

> "Character is doing the right thing when nobody's looking. There are too many people who think that the only thing that's right is to get by and the only thing that's wrong is to get caught." –J.C. WATTS

Jimmy had many jobs during his four years of high school, including selling seeds door to door, selling doughnuts in the school parking lot and delivering newspapers. He also worked as a pageboy at the Georgia Hotel and tried his hand at driving a truck – but it was Jimmy's passion for cars that paid off in the end. He started to buy and sell used cars via the classified ads in the newspaper and eventually landed himself a job with the Bowell McLean (BowMac) car dealership, where he worked for 10 years.

In 1961, Jimmy bought a Pontiac Buick dealership in Vancouver and started the company that would eventually grow to be the third-largest private company in Canada – with billions of dollars in annual revenue and 33,000 employees.

Jimmy credits his father with teaching him the value of honesty, not by what he said, but through his actions and his commitment to always do the right thing, even if it hurt. "My dad had a huge impact on me in terms of right and wrong," he told the students.

Who we become, our character, is something that is entirely up to us. We can be like Jimmy Pattison and take our cues from people we admire, like our parents. In the stories that follow, we'll explore what character is and why it's so important to your success in life.

CHAPTER 51

A MAN OF CHARACTER

C haracter is developed by living your principles. Over 2,500 years ago, a Chinese philosopher said, "Character is destiny." In an era where there is glory in narcissism and greed, does this still apply? To my mind, there is no higher praise than: He is a man a character.

Tong Louie was such a man. He lived his life wanting to be known as an ordinary, hardworking fellow and although hard work was the very essence of who he was, during his lifetime Tong demonstrated in a multitude of ways that he was, in fact, extraordinary.

According to his biographer, by the time he died at the age of 84, "Tong Louie was one of the leading industrialists in Western Canada, one of its most active philanthropists and a patriarch of one of its pioneering social groups."

As the second of 11 children born to Chinese immigrants, Tong learned early in life the values that would lead to his success. In 1934, his father, Hok Yat Louie (the "H.Y." in H.Y. Louie Co. Ltd.) wrote three letters to his sons while he was in Hong Kong and his sons were in Vancouver. His letters were simple truths that at the time were intended as guiding rules for the fledgling family business.

In his first letter he wrote:

"When pursuing prosperity, you must follow the rules of heaven. Don't be afraid to be kind and charitable . . . ill deeds should be avoided."

In his second letter, he told his sons to preserve their own reputations: "Be earnest, be fair and loyal in your dealings with customers."

And in his third, he imparted one last, precious lesson: "Develop your own character as well as your working skills."

For more than 60 years, Hok Yat's words have been a constant in the Louie family's success – incredibly simple and completely understandable advice that came from a father who cared not just about business, but about the importance of family, respect, community and living and working together.

Tong Louie built his life, career and character on those truths. In recognition of the extraordinary contributions he made to his community, he was awarded the Order of British Columbia, the Order of Canada, the Knight of the Golden

Pencil, the ASTRA Award and the Variety Club's Golden Heart Award.

Many of us are concerned about our reputation, but how many put as much emphasis on developing our character?

CHAPTER 52

CHARACTER IS AN INSIDE JOB

When it comes to character, there are three things I have learned from experience:

1. It is a waste of time trying to correct other people's mistakes. You must be the leader and set the example, but after that, it's up to each individual whether or not they choose to follow that example.

2. You can't change anybody else. People only change if they want to and each person must change themselves.

3. People are generally the way they are because they want to be and that goes for you and me too; we choose to be who we are.

The bottom line is people choose their own character, and although there is no end to the excuses we can come up with for why we would lie, cheat, steal, slack off, drink too much, take drugs, abuse our bodies, or any number of other destructive behaviours, the truth is we do things because we want to.

What will you do with your life?

Choose carefully. The decisions you make will have a profound effect on your career, the quality of your personal relationships and most importantly, what you see when you look in the mirror.

If we make the wrong choice, sooner or later it comes back to sting us – and sometimes it's a very big sting. Remember Bernie Madoff, the guy with the $50 billion Ponzi scheme? He's currently serving a 150-year prison sentence – the longest sentence they could give him. He wanted to be remembered as a titan of Wall Street; instead he'll go down as the biggest fraud of his time. Who knows what Madoff sees when he looks in the mirror, but I can't imagine it's a happy face smiling back. In a recent interview, Madoff's lawyer said that his wife Ruth stopped visiting him years ago and none of his grandchildren have come to see him since he's been in prison.

Sometimes it takes years, even decades, for poor character to catch up with us, but when it does, it wipes out everything good that came before. Consider these names as examples:

- O.J. Simpson
- Alan Eagleson (who was stripped of his Order of Canada and resigned from the Hockey Hall of Fame)
- Bill Cosby
- Ben Johnson

My mentor Ray Addington, who was President of Kelly Douglas Co. Ltd., often told me, "Not only must you do the right thing, but you must be seen to do the right thing."

John Maxwell says, "There is no such thing as 'business ethics' . . . it's all ethics!"

When you have integrity and hold yourself to a high standard of behaviour, all of the other values, such as honesty, loyalty, respect, accountability and compassion, naturally come along with it and you will find these traits attract people to you, engender trust and make them want to do business with you.

When you compromise integrity, a reputation that may have taken 25 years to build, can be destroyed in five minutes. Guard your reputation, it's the one thing that will follow you no matter where you go.

Here are five things that can ruin you:

1. Ego
2. Greed
3. Booze
4. Drugs
5. Illicit sex

I love this analogy from Mike Bechtle's book *You Can't Text a Tough Conversation*, which compares the development of good character with that of a healthy lawn.

As Mike explains, there are two parts to a healthy lawn: what's above the ground (visible to others) and what's below the ground (not visible to others). What happens below the ground determines what happens above the ground. "If we see wilted grass, we know the roots need more water. If the tips of the blades turn brown, it might mean they're getting too much water. If the grass looks dead, it might just be dormant. The key to a healthy lawn is to take care of what happens below ground." The same is true of people and our character. Whatever's going on within us eventually shows up on the outside where others can see it. If we want people to think highly of us and see us as someone of integrity, we have

> "A reputation, once damaged, may possibly be repaired, but the world will always keep their eyes on the spot where the crack was." —JOSEPH HALL.

to work on our character from within (underground) first. If we become a person of good character on the inside, that character will grow and flourish on the outside, where others can see it as well.

You can't fake character. If we're unhealthy on the inside, at some point it will show on the outside. Faking something is also a lot of work, and eventually the veneer cracks.

CHAPTER 53

7 SIGNS OF CHARACTERS

"Any fool can criticize, condemn and complain but it takes character and self control to be understanding and forgiving." —Dale Carnegie

C haracter isn't generally something we're born with. It comes from life experience and it's a result of the choices we make. Below are seven things we can work on to build our character every day.

Telling the truth
Telling a few white lies may seem harmless, but a study conducted by the University of Notre Dame suggests that you can improve your mental and physical health if you cut down on the fibbing. Using two groups of adults, the study tracked

how many lies the average person tells in a week (it's about 11) and then, using weekly questionnaires, measured the changes in mental and physical well-being that participants reported as they attempted to be more honest.

Over the course of the 10-week study, researchers found that not only were participants feeling better about themselves for being honest, they also stopped making excuses for things like being late or not finishing a task, and they developed strategies to avoid lying, like using questions to deflect in instances where they didn't want to answer a tough question.

Something else to keep in mind: lying is a lot of work. Once you've told a lie, you have to remember what you said and who you said it to. Telling the truth may not always be easy (some people prefer not to hear the truth) but it is far less complicated and in the end will save you a lot of anxiety.

A willingness to apologize

Making mistakes is part of being human; it's also part of learning. Being able to apologize and recognize when you may be wrong is probably one of the most important things in life. If you think you're never wrong, you're absolutely wrong about that. One of the things that makes apologizing so hard is that you're not just admitting to a failure, you're opening yourself up for the possibility that your apology will be turned down.

Avoiding shortcuts

It's tempting when you find a quick path to your goals, but more often than not it's worth it to take the long way around. Doing things the right way (often known as the hard way) builds up foundational skills and it also requires patience and self-control – two attributes that will serve you well in all areas of life.

Being kind

Kindness offered to the stranger passing by; in response to unkindness; or just because you can offer it is the sort of kindness that changes the world. As life gets busy and we start to forget about the little things, kindness is often the first to go. Make kindness a part of your day, every day. It's as simple as complimenting a colleague on

> **"When you have a bad day, a really bad day, try and treat the world better than it treated you."** —*PATRICK STUMP*

a job well done, sending a thank-you note, holding a door open or letting a car merge in front of you in traffic.

Taking one for the team

When an unwanted project is up for grabs, offering to handle it shows you're strong enough to take the hard stuff in stride. Volunteering to do the grunt work on a project you rank high enough to walk away from also demonstrates that you're more invested in the success of the team than you are in stroking your own ego.

Sharing credit

We've all had somebody take credit for something we worked on and felt the resentment grow inside of us. Not being recognized and thanked for our work is demoralizing. Sharing credit and thanking others for their contributions in public lets everyone know you're a value-added sort of person. Look for opportunities to give recognition for achievement, effort and character.

Forgiveness

This is a tough one for most of us. Psychologists define forgiveness as a conscious decision to release feelings of resentment or vengeance towards a person or group that has caused harm, regardless of whether or not they deserve it. However, that doesn't mean you have to deny the seriousness of the offense. Forgiveness does not mean forgetting, condoning or excusing – and although forgiveness can help repair a damaged relationship, it doesn't obligate you to reconcile with the person who harmed you, or release them from accountability. The purpose of forgiveness is to bring the

> **"The final forming of a person's character lies in their own hands."** —ANNE FRANK

forgiver peace of mind and free him or her from corrosive anger. In that way, it empowers you to recognize the pain you've suffered without letting that pain define you, so you can move on with your life.

CHAPTER 54

VW'S FALL FROM GRACE

"Good character is to be praised more than outstanding talent. Most talents are to some extent a gift. Good character, by contrast, is not given to us. We have to build it piece by piece, by thought, by choice, by courage and determination." —John Luther

L et's take a look at one of the biggest business scandals in recent memory. It took place in the automotive world.

Volkswagen is among the mightiest brands on the planet, but not too long ago the company got caught cheating.

The German automaker was forced to admit to installing onboard computer software in their vehicles designed to fool government emissions tests.

Volkswagen said, "This didn't happen in one day."

A *Globe and Mail* "Report on Business" story indicated, "Volkswagen executives are complicit in a massive cover-up at the highest levels."

Eleven million diesel cars were affected.

Volkswagen has been an iconic brand since the 1950s, when the Beetle went from ultra-niche to mainstream transportation. *Adweek* had recently called VW a brand that stood for quality, honesty and a commitment to its customers.

Aside from the impact on consumers who bought VW vehicles, think about how this wrongdoing has impacted the employees who work for the company and had no knowledge of what was happening. New Volkswagen CEO Matthias Mueller warned staff to brace for cutbacks in response to the diesel emissions scandal, which also hammered the company's stock price.

"We need to make massive cutbacks in order to manage the consequences of the crisis," Mueller told VW's 20,000-plus workers at a staff gathering. Mueller said the company's most important task was to restore trust. But how do you do that when you've just admitted that you rigged the emissions controls on 11 million vehicles? By the way, more than eight million of those were in the European Union and the remainder in North America and beyond, so this deception spans continents.

It doesn't take much to destroy a legacy, or a reputation.

In one news report, there was a claim by VW that only three staff members were behind the scandal – but that's a bit hard to believe.

This whole issue is about character, or should I say lack of character and leadership, and a belief that no one would find out. That is why character is so important.

The valuation of VW's stock dropped almost $20 billion and thousands of employees stood to lose their jobs as a result, not to mention all of the associated companies around the world that have been impacted by the loss.

Let me ask you this: Do you think those responsible for this massive worldwide deceit would like to go back a few years and rethink their decision?

Chris Woodyard, who writes for *USA Today* and specializes in the automotive industry, wrote: "In the end, the automaker finds itself in crisis, all because it lost sight of the values that led to its greatness. Maybe it's time to think small all over again."

As Roy Disney says, "When values are clear, decision-making is easy."

If the choices the folks at VW were making had come from a place of strong character, which includes values like integrity, honesty and truthfulness, I am sure we would not be talking about this.

In contrast to what happened with VW and how they responded once the cat was out of the bag, you might remember the Tylenol scandal back in 1982. Someone had tampered with bottles of Tylenol in the Chicago area. Seven people died and it was eventually discovered that it was because a number of Tylenol capsules had been laced with cyanide.

James Burke, CEO of Johnson & Johnson, made a very quick decision to remove all Tylenol bottles off every shelf in the United States – every single bottle!

Initially, the company's stock plummetted and it cost the company $100 million to relaunch, but two months later the stock recovered and actually rose in value, all because a decision had been made based on character, not fear, with the ultimate goal being to protect the population and make them feel secure, and confident in the product.

Johnson & Johnson never looked back.

We live in a world where it seems that scandals are reported daily – on CNN, in the *Wall Street Journal*, *Vancouver Sun*, *Globe and Mail*. Whether it's a government agency that won't pursue high-net-worth tax evaders, a drug company that fixes prices on lifesaving medication, shadow flipping in the real estate industry, or politicians who charge personal expenses to the taxpayers – decisions are made every day with no regard for morality or character. Yes, we all make mistakes from time to time, but that's not the same as a blatant disregard for doing the right thing. Imagine having your next surgery performed by a doctor who cheated his or her way through medical school. How about trusting your life savings with a financial adviser who never actually does any due diligence before placing client money into a new investment?

Build your integrity and be known as a person of character.

CHAPTER 55

A CONFERENCE ON CHARACTER

"There are character-defining moments in each of our lives. The choices we make, what we say or do and how we treat others define our character, moment by moment . . ." —Senator Yonah Martin

The first Character Canada Conference was held in Abbotsford last October with hundreds of people in attendance, and I was honoured to be one of the speakers. The purpose of the conference is to bring people from communities across Canada together to promote leadership, positive values and community involvement.

The six values identified as being integral to character are: respect, responsibility, integrity, empathy, courage and service.

Following the event, the chair of the Conference Planning Committee, Vijay Manuel, shared his reflections on the conference and why it is integral to focus on character. The one below is my favourite because I think it sums up why character is so much more important than reputation.

"It's not about being perfect, we all make mistakes. Perhaps our response to the mistakes we make is the biggest indicator of the depth of our character."

So what is character? It is the core of your being, it is who you are. Good character is a commitment to do what is wise, honest and right, regardless of the cost or circumstances.

The aforementioned John C. Maxwell said: "The average person directly or indirectly influences 10,000 other people during his or her lifetime and those who are in leadership influence many, many more."

So who is watching you? You might be surprised.

- Your spouse
- Your children
- Your co-workers
- Your suppliers
- Your customers
- Your neighbours
- Your community
- Your friends

Virtually any person or organization you come in contact

with may be watching; so what do they see?

Here are a few of the things that I believe show good character:

- Being willing to take a stand for what is right, even when others don't back you up.
- Having great conviction for doing what is right, especially when it is not convenient to do it.
- Knowing there is always something to be thankful for and appreciating what you have.
- Treating others as you would like to be treated.
- Putting others first.
- Speaking the truth.

The greatest power we possess is the power to make our own life a shining example for others in the hope that we might inspire them to do the same. "Example is not the main thing in influencing others," said Albert Schweitzer. "It is the only thing." Whether you are a business owner, employee, educator or entrepreneur, you can lead with character within your spheres of influence to inspire those around you to do the same.

CHAPTER 56

NOT FOR THE
FAINT OF HEART

G eoff Brooks is a strategic partnership specialist at
Canada Wide Media Limited.

Not too long ago, he announced that he was going
to spend an evening on the streets in Vancouver as part of "A
Night in the Life," a program organized by Directions Youth
Services Centre under Family Services of Greater Vancouver.

The object is both to raise awareness of homeless youth
and money for the essential work that Family Services does.

Raising $4,000 was an easier task than spending a night
on the streets.

I asked Geoff to recount this unique journey for the rest of
us. Here is his story:

* * * * * * *

As I had expected, it was an eye-opening and humbling experience. I was extremely nervous anticipating the evening, but was comforted by the homeless youth, youth workers and fellow participants as soon as I signed in. The youth were well spoken, passionate about their community, and excited for the opportunity to tell us about their lives.

They led us on a tour of the streets, showing us places to sleep and find shelter, places they can safely feed their addictions and a popular spot to earn some money by squeegy-ing cars or begging. We visited the north side of the Burrard Street Bridge, a popular place to rest for the night. It is out of the way; the police and the public don't bother them here and they can sleep in groups for safety.

They pointed out the community gardens as a popular spot nearby. They're constantly moving around the city and they keep those movements quite random to avoid their belongings going missing or risking abuse while they sleep.

Comparatively, the streets are one of the safer options for some semblance of shelter. I learned a bit about the shelter system and SROs – single-room occupancy hotels. They're apparently dangerous, unkempt and extremely unsanitary, with shared washrooms; a place employed for drug use hours on end. One youth described a recent experience of catching on fire during a night's stay (I didn't ask how). By the time she got to an unoccupied washroom to quell the flames, she was naked, swarmed by other residents and covered with second-degree burns. She then endured physical rehab for months and found appropriate short-term housing, but found herself back in an SRO – where infections plagued her recovery. Despite that experience, she was a seemingly bright, 20-something homeless youth volunteer who wanted to share her experience with us.

After the tour of the streets, we were invited to enjoy some soup served from the kitchen at Directions. I chatted to a few youth workers, some of whom have battled homelessness and addictions themselves. They relate well with the youth and provide necessary peer-to-peer support. They then introduced us to the "homelessness simulator," which took us throughout the Directions facility.

We were each given a profile (I was an underage young woman named Marisol with addictions and a dog). The goal was to eat three meals and also find employment and housing before the 90-minute session was over. The intent was to show us the barriers and difficulty involved in the everyday process of life as a homeless youth.

Here's a glimpse of the experience. If you don't have any money, you can't take the bus to get to the employment assistance office to get a job and earn an income. When you find a social worker who gives you bus money, you learn that dogs are not welcome in government offices. A trip to Directions is necessary to drop your dog off for the short term,

*which means another trip on the bus that you can't afford.
When you return to the employment office, you learn that
with a history of addiction, it is difficult to find employment
without a visit to a doctor. Meanwhile, the police (played by
a few homeless youth themselves, who never broke character)
made it more difficult by arresting you for loitering outside
of the employment office. The office seemed to have very
limited hours of operation. If you don't have ID on you
(which is a reality for many homeless), all these simple tasks
become nearly impossible, inviting more harassment from
the authorities. Because I was an underaged female, it was
impossible to find an appropriate shelter for the evening.
Out of desperation, I had to find a way to spend the last few
minutes of the exercise in jail, as that was the best option for
shelter for the night.*

*The youth then shared real-life stories, including tales of
abuse in shelters, struggling to survive, transit nightmares,
fines, the necessity of political support, and whispers of the
generational effect of abuse at Aboriginal residential schools.*

*Any rest we got while sleeping on the streets was short-
lived. I managed to shut my eyes for an hour, but was
interrupted by youth wondering why we got to sleep out front
and they didn't. Other youth coming to use Directions' services
understood and appreciated what we were doing. However,
being across from St. Paul's Hospital's emergency department,
there were plenty of sirens to keep us up as well. My cardboard*

mattress wasn't the most comfortable, but it was dry and the area was well lit.

We were up and out by 5 a.m., with a bit more perspective and appreciation for a nice warm bed and a roof over our heads. As I enjoyed the luxury of a taxi home for a few more hours of sleep, the thought of 700 to 1,000 youth spending their night outside, in all sorts of weather and a nearly impossible lifestyle, was simply unfathomable.

CHAPTER 57

IT'S BIGGER THAN
YOU AND ME

I noticed this year that Earth Day, which is credited with helping launch the modern environmental movement, is getting a lot more mainstream awareness. One of the great paradoxes of life is that we are divided from one another by geography, nationality, our beliefs, our professions, and a hundred other little things, and yet, in a larger sense, we are all united. We all breathe the same air and rely on the same water for our existence. Whatever we do or don't do has an impact on the lives of others (and as we are coming to realize, all life on the planet). Therefore, we have a certain responsibility to each other to do what is best, whether we like it or not.

Often in our busy, fragmented lives it can be easy to overlook the fact that we are part of something greater than ourselves – a community, humankind, inhabitants of Planet Earth. Because of our tendency to forget this, we find it easy to make decisions that don't reflect that responsibility, focusing instead on our immediate wants and needs without worrying about the long-term consequences. It's also easy to shy away from serving the greater good because it seems like "hard work." The challenge we all face is to expand our minds beyond making distinctions between ourselves and others, so we are aware of how our choices can and do impact a greater cause.

Happily contributing to the greater good isn't all about self-sacrifice. For example, if you plant a tree in your community, it will shade and protect you as well as your neighbours (and also remove carbon from the atmosphere, making it a win-win-win scenario). When we serve the greater community, we also serve our own greater good. When we internalize that, we become aware of our power and ability to influence and create positive change in the world.

Collectively, we can do great things. Embrace your interdependency.

CHAPTER 58

THE MAGICAL, MYSTICAL LISTICLE

The Internet is obsessed with listicles and on some popular sites the majority of stories are written in this format, with titles like "The 10 Places You Have to See Before You Die." There's something about a list that gets our attention; maybe it's the fact that, as humans, we're curious animals and we need to know what's on the list. Or perhaps it's the sense that we'll be missing out if we don't know the 10 places we absolutely *have* to see before shuffling off this mortal coil. (What if it turns out we've only been to seven?)

The New Yorker ran a story a few years ago on why we love lists. The article explained that our brains are attracted to information that has already been organized and digested for us. "It spatially organizes the information and promises a story whose length has been quantified up front. Together, these create an easy reading experience, in which the mental heavy lifting of conceptualization, categorization and analysis is completed well in advance of actual consumption – a bit like sipping green juice instead of munching on a bundle of kale. And there's little that our brains crave more than effortlessly acquired data."

There's also plenty of evidence that we retain information better when it is presented in a list, because lists appeal to our general tendency to organize and categorize things. For example, it's hard to memorize the groceries we need to buy if we don't write them down, but once we've made a list on a piece of paper, even if we forget that paper at home, it is easier for us to recall what was on it because we can think back to the location of the words on the page.

Here's my own take on the listicle:

Five Things You Need to Give Up to Be Successful

Give up blame.
When you blame other people or forces for what's happening in your life, you give up your power. Even if you can't control what's happening, you can decide how you're going to respond to what's happening and how much impact you will allow it

to have. By taking responsibility for yourself, you have the power to choose.

Give up your resistance to change.

There is one constant in life: things change. And change is good. It presents you with new options and possibilities. It also provides opportunities to grow, try different ways of doing things and even totally reinvent yourself. It's stressful to try to keep things the same; when you embrace change, it's much easier to go with the flow.

Give up that self-defeating voice in your head.

A little self-criticism is a good thing: It can be a reality check that spurs you to be a better person, but don't believe everything your mind tells you, especially if it is consistently negative and self-defeating. If the voice in your head is putting you down and making you feel like you're never good enough, it's time to tell it to hush up. Negative self-talk isn't motivating; instead, it leads us to focus on our failures and lose sight of the things we're doing right. Something you might want to try is reframing negative thoughts into action.

Rather than thinking, "I am a disorganized slob," try: "I've really let my office get out of control, but if I do a little every day, I can sort it out and get back on top of it." A good rule of thumb with your thoughts is, if you wouldn't say it to your friend, don't say it to yourself.

Give up the need to be right.

Every human has a unique set of DNA, which means that every brain is wired differently, so what makes sense to you, won't necessarily make sense for me. Does that mean you're right and I'm wrong? Or I'm right and you're wrong, just because you think differently from me? I hope not.

Unfortunately, the need to be right fuels many of the worst conflicts on the planet. Rigid ideas and opinions keep us from trying new things, learning from others and evolving. Needing to be right comes at a heavy price. People who have to be right cut themselves off from what the world has to offer because they are convinced they know best, but in the end they are the ones who suffer most.

Give up waiting for the perfect moment.

Do you find yourself saying things like, "I'd love to start my own business, I'm just waiting until . . ."? The thing you're waiting for is the perfect moment, but it never arrives. There's always some reason, some excuse why it's not quite the right time – and it never will be, because that's your fear talking. If you let it, fear will keep you holding off on your ambition forever. There is no other moment. This is not a dress rehearsal, this is life. *This* is your moment. Get out there and make it happen, whatever "it" might be.

CHAPTER 59

YOU NEVER KNOW

As Mrs. Thompson stood in front of her fifth-grade class on the very first day of school, she told the children an untruth. Like most teachers, she looked at her students and said that she loved them all the same. However, that was impossible, because there in the front row, slumped in his seat, was a little boy named Teddy Stoddard.

Mrs. Thompson had watched Teddy the year before and noticed that he did not play well with the other children, that his clothes were messy and that he constantly needed a bath. In addition, Teddy could be unpleasant. It got to the point where Mrs. Thompson would actually delight in marking his papers with a broad red pen, making bold X's and then putting a big "F" at the top of the page.

At the school where Mrs. Thompson taught, she was required to review each child's past records; she put Teddy's off until last. However, when she did finally sit down to go over his file, she was in for a surprise.

Teddy's first-grade teacher wrote, "Teddy is a bright child with a ready laugh. He does his work neatly and has good manners . . . he is a joy to be around."

His second-grade teacher wrote, "Teddy is an excellent student, well-liked by his classmates, but he is troubled because his mother has a terminal illness and life at home must be a struggle."

His third-grade teacher wrote, "His mother's death has been hard on him. He tries to do his best, but his father doesn't show much interest, and his home life will soon affect him if some steps aren't taken."

Teddy's fourth-grade teacher wrote, "Teddy is withdrawn and doesn't show much interest in school. He doesn't have many friends and he sometimes sleeps in class."

By now, Mrs. Thompson realized the problem and she was ashamed of herself. She felt even worse when her students brought her Christmas presents, wrapped in beautiful ribbons and bright paper, except for Teddy's. His present was clumsily wrapped in the heavy brown paper that he got from a grocery bag. Mrs. Thompson took pains to open it in the middle of the other presents. Some of the children started to laugh when she found a rhinestone bracelet with some of the stones missing, and a bottle that was one-quarter full of perfume. But she stifled the children's laughter when she exclaimed how pretty the bracelet was, putting it on, and dabbing some of the perfume on her wrist. Teddy Stoddard stayed after school that day just long enough to say, "Mrs. Thompson, today you smelled just like my mom used to."

After the children left, she cried for at least an hour. On that very day, she quit teaching reading, writing and arithmetic. Instead, she began to teach children. Mrs. Thompson paid particular attention to Teddy. As she worked with him, his mind seemed to come alive. The more she encouraged him, the faster he responded. By the end of the year, Teddy had become one of the top students in the class and, despite her lie that she would love all the children the same, Teddy became one of her "teacher's pets."

A year later, she found a note under her door, from Teddy, telling her that she was the best teacher he ever had in his whole life.

Six years went by before she got another note from Teddy. He then wrote that he had finished high school, third in his class, and that she was still the best teacher he'd ever had.

Four years after that, she got another letter, saying that while things had been tough at times, he'd stayed in school, had stuck with it, and would soon graduate from college with the highest of honours. And still, he'd never had a better teacher than Mrs. Thompson.

Then four more years passed and yet another letter came. This time he explained that after he got his bachelor's degree, he decided to go a little further. The letter ended, as usual, by explaining that she was still the best and favourite teacher he'd ever had. But now the name at the end was a little longer; the letter was signed, Theodore F. Stoddard, MD.

The story does not end there. You see, there was yet another letter that spring. Teddy said he had met a girl and was going to be married. He explained that his father had died a couple of years ago and he was wondering if Mrs. Thompson might agree to sit at the wedding in the place that was usually reserved for the mother of the groom. Of course, Mrs. Thompson did. And guess what? She wore that bracelet, the one with the missing rhinestones. Moreover, she made sure she was wearing the perfume that Teddy remembered his mother wearing on their last Christmas together.

They hugged each other and Dr. Stoddard whispered in Mrs. Thompson's ear, "Thank you, Mrs. Thompson, for believing in me. Thank you so much for making me feel important and showing me that I could make a difference."

Mrs. Thompson, with tears in her eyes, whispered back, "Teddy, you have it all wrong. You were the one who taught me that I could make a difference. I didn't know how to teach until I met you."

You never fully know where a kind word, a simple gesture, a voice of encouragement can impact someone else for good.

Plato once said, "Be kind to everyone, because everyone you meet is fighting a hard battle." And 98 per cent is hidden from view.

CHAPTER 60

HOW TO COMMUNICATE EFFECTIVELY (WHEN YOU JUST WANT TO SCREAM)

I like Winnipeg, Manitoba: its big, blue prairie sky; friendly, welcoming people; and the positive way the city gets things done.

What's positive in Winnipeg, you ask? Everything from a self-deprecating joke about the city's famous mosquitoes that rise in black clouds each summer from the flatland waterways, to hearing from a fur-covered, frost-encrusted Winnipeg veteran that he's proud to be living in the world's "biggest coldest" city (until fairly recently, it held the record for being the chilliest city in the world with a population over 600,000). That's not just talking positive, it's a manifestation of raw courage.

On a sparkling spring day when the last of the winter had gone and the sun flashed up at the aircraft from pools of melted snow below us, I flew into Winnipeg to make a speech.

I was on a ridiculous schedule at the time. Upon landing, I would grab a cab at the airport, head downtown, make the speech, mingle with the delegates at a conference, sleep, head back to the airport and hop on a plane through Toronto to London, England – where I would do the same thing all over again.

Before leaving the Winnipeg airport to head downtown, I went up to the Air Canada counter, gave them my name and schedule and said to the attendant: "I'm staying at the Westin. It's very important that I be in London tomorrow night. If there are any flight changes, could you please let me know?" He assured me he would.

With confidence – and nice feelings about the assignment ahead – I took the cab downtown, made the speech, mingled a bit and went to bed. I got up the next morning and got a cab to the airport to catch the flight that would get me to London. It was another lovely morning.

I walked to the counter, slapped down my ticket and passport and said, "Good morning."

The attendant looked down at my ticket, then looked up at me and informed me that the flight had been cancelled.

You know the feeling you get in a situation like that. The

blood moves from the top of your forehead, you drop your shoulders, you assume a fighting, protective stance – a kill-anyone stance. It's a reaction that's latent in all of us; it's human nature.

But we can control it.

Miraculously, the reasoning side of my brain clicked in at that moment.

"Peter," it said, "whatever has happened is probably not the fault of this Air Canada attendant and it will not do you any good at all to blow up, ruin his day and still not get to London."

So I said to the agent, "I wish you had called me at the hotel, I *did* leave a number."

"Yes sir, I know you did," he said. "But the cancellation came just a short time ago and we didn't have the manpower to inform all of our passengers."

"Well, no problem," I answered. "You can put me on another flight to Toronto and I can still connect to London."

"There are no other flights to Toronto, sir," he informed me.

I took a deep breath to stabilize my heartbeat and that reasoning side of my brain chimed in again.

"Whatever is happening is not the fault of this attendant, Peter," it told me. "And it will not do you any good at all to blow up, ruin his day and still not get to London."

So I turned to the agent and said, "Is there *any* way at all you can help me get to London today?"

There was a note in my voice that I rarely hear. It comes from way down deep in the pleading part of our anatomy and that, too, is part of the evolution of mankind.

"Just a moment, sir," he said and left the counter.

I stood there half fuming and half in a panic, waiting until he returned – a full 20 minutes later!

"Mr. Legge," he said. "Here's what I've done."

I knew at that moment that he had solved the problem and I leaned on the counter and listened intently as he explained.

"In 20 minutes you will be leaving on a plane for Calgary."

"Yes," I said.

"An hour after you get to Calgary, you will be connecting with an Air Canada flight out of Vancouver, which, despite some headwinds over Greenland this afternoon, will get you to London just two hours later than the original flight you were hoping to take through Toronto, OK?"

I reached across the counter, grabbed his hand and shook it gratefully as I read the name on his lapel, then replied, "Thank you, John. Thank you."

CHAPTER 61

THE TRIPLE FILTER TEST

The tongue can be a vicious tool – be careful how you use it. The very wise Socrates had an interesting take on gossip: unless it's the absolute truth, you should probably keep it to yourself. The following was sent my way by a colleague. The Triple Filter Test is a good reminder of how to deal with gossip as we encounter it.

In ancient Greece (469 - 399 BC), Socrates was widely lauded for his wisdom. One day, an acquaintance ran up to him excitedly and said, "Socrates, do you know what I just heard about Diogenes?"

"Wait a moment," Socrates replied. "Before you tell me, I'd like you to pass a little test. It's called the Triple Filter Test."

"Triple filter?" asked the acquaintance.

"That's right," Socrates continued. "Before you talk to me about Diogenes, let's take a moment to filter what you're going to say. The first filter is Truth. Have you made absolutely sure that what you are about to tell me is true?"

"No," the man said. "Actually, I just heard about it."

"All right," said Socrates. "So you don't really know if it's true or not. Now let's try the second filter, the filter of Goodness. Is what you are about to tell me about Diogenes something good?"

"No, on the contrary . . ."

"So," Socrates continued, "you want to tell me something about Diogenes that may be bad, even though you're not certain it's true?"

The man shrugged, a little embarrassed. Socrates continued, "You may still pass the test though, because there is a third filter, the filter of Usefulness. Is what you want to tell me about Diogenes going to be useful to me?"

"No, not really."

"Well," concluded Socrates, "if what you want to tell me is likely neither True nor Good nor even Useful, why tell it to me, or anyone at all?"

The man was bewildered and ashamed.

This is an example of why Socrates was a great philosopher and held in such high esteem.

CHAPTER 62

THE FORTUNATE ONES

*"In ordinary life we hardly realize that we receive
a great deal more than we give and that it is only with gratitude
that life becomes rich."* —Dietrich Bonhoeffer

We live in a country where the majority of people are what I would call over-privileged and logically you would think that would make us endlessly thankful for what we have – especially if we happen to pay attention to what is going on in the rest of the world. But more often than not, we feel entitled to even more.

Whenever I speak to an audience about how much abundance we have in our lives, I always say that we can all come up with at least 15 things to be grateful for. When we are verbally grateful for the blessings in our life, it changes everything: our perspective on how much we need, our sense of entitlement, and most importantly, it changes our attitude. Consider this:

- If you woke up this morning with more health than illness, you are more blessed than the millions who will not survive the week.
- If you have never experienced the danger of battle, the loneliness of imprisonment, the agony of torture or the pangs of starvation, you are more fortunate than 500 million people the world over.
- If you can attend a religious meeting without fear of harassment, arrest, torture or death, you are more blessed than three billion people in the world.
- If you have enough food to eat, clothes on your back, a roof overhead and a place to sleep, you are richer than 75 per cent of the world.

> "Piglet noticed that even though he had a very small heart, it could hold a rather large amount of gratitude."—A.A. MILNE
> (FROM WINNIE-THE-POOH)

- If you have money in the bank, in your wallet and spare change in a dish someplace, you are among the top eight per cent of the world's wealthy.
- If you hold up your head with a smile on your face and are truly thankful, you are blessed – because the majority can, but most choose not to.

- If you can hold someone's hand, hug them or even pat them on the shoulder, you are blessed because you can offer a healing touch.

Never forget that you are one of the fortunate ones. Count your blessings every day and soon you too will realize just how privileged you truly are.

CHAPTER 63

INVEST IN YOUR MIND

I am often asked if I really do read one book a week and, if so, how do I do it? Well, yes, I do. In fact, these past 30 years, I have read 1,500 books; mostly biographies, sales books, books on speaking and on leadership, just to name a few.

The real question is, do you think it has helped me in my career? Absolutely!

It all began for me when Arizona speaker Joel Weldon encouraged me to read 17 pages a day or approximately one book a month, which equals 12 books a year; that started me on this quest.

I believe reading is an investment in yourself. It's also an investment in your brain, your memory and your health as you grow older. After I had my stroke, my doctor stopped by my hospital bed to talk about the images of my brain. He'd noticed that although I had suffered damage, my brain actually had the appearance of someone much younger than my chronological age and he was trying to understand why. After asking my wife a series of questions, he inquired about my reading habits and Kay told him I am, in fact, a voracious reader.

"That's it!" he said. "That's what's keeping his brain young."

For me, reading is about much more than just entertainment or racking up an impressive number of books read. Reading allows me to keep learning, it introduces me to fascinating people I'll never meet and challenges me with new ideas. If you develop the same habit of reading, I promise you will never be the same again.

Here are my tips for anyone who wants to read more:

- Turn off all your electronics for an hour at night and read.
- Read in the mornings for a half-hour.
- Read on the plane if you're travelling and read again a half-hour before bed.
- Build up a reading list and purchase the books on your list so you always have something to look forward to.
- Join a book club – these days there are clubs for every interest (biography, popular fiction, non-fiction).
- Make sure you always have a new book to take with you when you go on vacation.
- Create a special space in your home for reading to make it

somewhere you want to spend more time.

- Read with your children, grandchildren, nieces and nephews; books are more enjoyable when they are shared, and reading is an activity that inspires calmness and reflection.

Thirty minutes a day could change your life. Challenge yourself to read something useful, challenging or educational every day. Thirty minutes spent with a book that motivates, excites or educates you will make a world of difference. Charles Scribner said, "Reading is a means of thinking with another person's mind; it forces you to stretch your own."

But don't stop at reading; share the wealth and share the wisdom. Send articles to friends and business associates. When you find topical information that you think might help someone else, don't hesitate to pass it along. We could all use a little boost now and then in terms of new ideas. It's also a great way to motivate staff or give a friend or family member extra encouragement.

You could also join a discussion group (in person or online) to share ideas with people around the world, opening your mind to even more perspectives on what you are learning. Taking it a step further, you could keep a journal for your thoughts and ideas and try to carry it with you so you can add insights that come your way throughout the day. This notebook will help you track your progress and make your learning more tangible, in addition to being a place where you can record inspiring quotes for future reference and keep a list of books you want to read in the future.

Benjamin Franklin, Bill Gates, Warren Buffet, Mark Zuckerberg, Oprah Winfrey, Arthur Blank (founder of Home Depot), Dan Gilbert (owner of the Cleveland Cavaliers) and no doubt countless others have all subscribed to the habit of reading at least one hour a day.

As the old saying goes: if it's good enough for these billionaires, then it must be good enough for you and me.

> **"It's not the cost of the book. It's what it may cost you not to buy and read it."**
> *— JIM ROHN*

CHAPTER 64

COURTESY CHECKLIST

I was browsing the Internet when I came across a blog where a group of people had been discussing the topic of courtesy in modern times. One of them provided the following definition of courtesy, which I quite liked: "Courtesy is the ability to acknowledge in a friendly way the human dignity of those around you, whatever the circumstances."

Courtesy is so important to me and how my company does business, that the last thing I do before I hire a senior-level person is to take them out for lunch to observe their manners and how they treat restaurant staff throughout the meal. It gives me a good indication of how they will treat my customers and the staff who will work for them.

Here are some questions to help you check your courtesy quotient:

- Do you return phone calls and emails in a timely manner?
- Do you regularly express gratitude to those around you, especially when someone has done something nice for you?
- Are you available to others without making them feel like they're imposing?
- Do you make sure never to keep people waiting more than a few minutes to meet you?
- Have you trained your staff to respond with courtesy and politeness in all situations?
- Do you regularly ask others for input on issues that concern them, and then genuinely consider what they have offered?
- Do you open the door for others or hold the door for those entering behind you?
- Do you always say please and thank you at restaurants, when you shop or when someone has helped you in some way or extended you a courtesy?
- Do you shut off your cellphone or set it to vibrate when you are meeting with someone?
- Do you allow the person with only one item to go ahead of you at the check-out?
- Do you conduct yourself in a polite manner when someone has made a mistake and you are contacting them to get it sorted out?

- Do you allow other vehicles to move into the lane in front of you without honking your horn at them or becoming angry and aggressive?
- Do you pay your bills on time, or let your creditors know if you cannot?
- Do you make sure never to put down your competitors or speak ill of them?
- Do you make every effort to hold your tongue when you feel like flying off the handle?

While all of these niceties may seem like small things – it really is the small gestures we make towards others that leave a lasting impression. If you're not sure how you measure up, do a courtesy check on yourself.

CHAPTER 65

APPRECIATE EACH DAY

Earlier this year, I celebrated my 74th birthday, and while I'm in good health, have lots of energy and am very active, I realize there's more road behind me than ahead of me. Life is racing for all of us. So today, I'd like you to read through these 12 affirmations that were emailed to me by my longtime accountant and friend Bryan Locke.

They are quotes from people who have realized that life is a fleeting commodity:

1. Today, I interviewed my grandmother as part of a research paper I'm working on for my psychology class. When I asked her to define success in her own words, she said, "Success is when you look back at your life and the memories make you smile."

2. Today, I asked my mentor, who is a very successful businessman in his 70s, what his top three tips are for success. He smiled and said, "Read something no one else is reading, think something no one else is thinking and do something no one else is doing."

3. Today, after a 72-hour shift at the fire station, a woman ran up to me at the grocery store and gave me a hug. When I tensed up, she realized I didn't recognize her. She let go with tears of joy in her eyes and the most sincere smile and said, "On September 11, 2001, you carried me out of the World Trade Center."

4. Today, after I watched my dog get run over by a car, I sat on the side of the road holding him and crying and just before he died, he licked the tears off my face.

5. Today at 7 a.m., I woke up feeling ill but decided I needed the money, so I went in to work. At 3 p.m., I got laid off. On my drive home I got a flat tire. When I went into the trunk for the spare, it was flat too. A man in a BMW pulled over and gave me a ride, we chatted and then he offered me a job. I start tomorrow.

6. Today, as my father, three brothers and two sisters stood around my mother's hospital bed, my mother uttered her last coherent words before she died. She simply said, "I feel so loved right now. We should have gotten together like this more often."

7. Today, I kissed my dad on the forehead as he passed away in a small hospital bed. About five seconds after he passed, I realized it was the first time I had given him a kiss since I was a little boy.

8. Today, in the cutest voice, my eight-year-old daughter asked me to start recycling. I chuckled and asked, "Why?" She replied, "So you can help me save the planet." I chuckled again and asked, "And why do you want to save the planet?" "Because that's where I keep all my stuff," she said.

9. Today, when I witnessed a 27-year-old breast cancer patient laughing hysterically at her two-year-old daughter's antics, I suddenly realized that I need to stop complaining about my life and start celebrating it again.

10. Today, a boy in a wheelchair saw me desperately struggling on crutches with my broken leg and offered to carry my backpack and books for me. He helped me all the way across campus to my class and as he was leaving he said, "I hope you feel better soon."

11. Today, I was feeling down because the results of a biopsy came back malignant. When I got home, I opened an email that said, "Thinking of you today. If you need me, I'm a phone call away." It was from a high school friend I hadn't seen in 10 years.

12. Today, I was travelling in Kenya and I met a refugee from Zimbabwe. He said he hadn't eaten anything in over three days, and looked extremely skinny and unhealthy. Then my friend offered him the rest of the sandwich he was eating. The first thing the man said was, "We can share it?"

CHAPTER 66

OBSTACLE OR OPPORTUNITY?

T he Royal Palace in Tehran, Iran, contains what is undoubtedly one of the most beautiful mosaic master-pieces in the world. The interior walls and ceiling sparkle with multifaceted reflections, as if encrusted with thousands upon thousands of diamonds. However, this vision of beauty is not quite what it was originally intended to be.

When the palace was first designed, the architect in charge specified that huge sheets of mirrors should hang on the walls. Unfortunately, when the first shipment of mirrors arrived from Paris, the builders discovered that the glass had been shattered in transit. The head contractor promptly threw the mirrors in the trash and sadly informed the architect of the problem.

To the surprise of the builders, the architect didn't despair at this news. Instead, he ordered that all of the broken pieces be gathered together and brought to him. He then proceeded to smash the glass into even smaller pieces which would be glued onto the walls, creating an indelible shimmering mosaic.

Obviously, the architect had the eye of an artist to be able to take something broken and turn it into a masterpiece. However, there is another lesson to be gleaned from the story and it is this: If we simply choose to see things from a different angle, what looks like an obstacle to success can in fact be a glorious opportunity.

Obstacles are a fact of life, we all encounter them. What's important is how we deal with them. When you're presented with an obstacle, step back for a moment and try to see how you can turn it to your advantage.

CHAPTER 67

DON'T WAIT
FOR THE BRICK

A young, successful executive was driving home, going a bit too fast in his new Jaguar. Suddenly, a brick came flying out and smashed into the Jag's side panel. He slammed on the brakes and reversed the car. Seeing a kid standing on the road, the angry driver jumped out, grabbed the kid and pushed him up against a parked car, shouting, "What was that all about? Just what the heck are you doing? That's a new car and that brick you threw is going to cost a lot of money. Why did you do it?"

"Please mister, I'm sorry, I didn't know what else to do," the young boy pleaded. "I threw the brick because no one else would stop."

With tears dripping down his face, he pointed to a spot just around another parked car. "It's my brother," he said. "He rolled off the curb and fell out of his wheelchair."

Sobbing, the boy asked the stunned executive, "Would you please help me get him back into his wheelchair? He's hurt and he's too heavy for me."

The driver tried to swallow the lump rising in his throat as he lifted the brother back into the wheelchair, then took out his fancy handkerchief and dabbed at the fresh scrapes and cuts on his arms and legs. A quick look told him everything was going to be OK.

"Thank you," the grateful child told the stranger.

Too shaken up for words, the man simply watched the little boy push his wheelchair-bound brother down the sidewalk. It was a long, slow walk back to the Jaguar. The damage was noticeable, but the driver decided to keep the dent as a reminder not to go through life so fast that someone would have to throw another brick just to get his attention.

The same applies to each one of us: we can slow down and pay attention . . . or wait for the brick.

CHAPTER 68

DON'T GET WRAPPED UP IN YOURSELF

As I mention elsewhere in this book, I learned a lot from my friendship with big band leader Dal Richards, but two things that stand out for me are his down-to-earth approach and his humility. Dal always said, "No matter how much fame and fortune you achieve, don't get wrapped up in yourself."

There was a point in my own life when I lost sight of this important lesson. Thankfully, an experience in the community of Williams Lake set me straight.

During my speaking career, I've jetted around in some of the best seats, performed in amazing international venues, checked into luxurious hotels and been served the finest food and wine. On one such occasion, I was scheduled to speak in Vienna, Austria, and my hosts spared no expense, arranging to fly both myself and my wife first class and provide a suite at a posh hotel where our every whim was catered to. I'll tell you, it isn't difficult to become accustomed to that sort of lifestyle.

And then I was invited to speak at the annual meeting of the Cattlemen's Association in the small town of Williams Lake, B.C.

I asked the booking agent if they would be flying me in a jet.

"Certainly!" she responded.

Picking me up in a limo?

"Of course," she assured me.

Would I be speaking at the convention centre?

"Absolutely!"

With a state-of-the-art sound system?

"Most assuredly!"

Satisfied, I accepted the engagement.

As it turned out, the private jet was a Dash 8 on a milk run. When I arrived at the airport, there was no one waiting at the gate to meet me and as the small terminal quickly cleared and I walked outside, it was obvious that there was no limo either, just a dusty yellow minibus idling at the curb.

"I'm expecting a limo," I told the driver who was waiting beside the bus.

"You must be Mr. Legge," he said smiling. "Hop in, this is your limousine."

I took a seat and we bumped along into town, but instead of arriving at the convention centre, the bus pulled up in front of the local arena. Apparently, this was to be my speaking venue. As for the state-of-the-art sound system, it was nothing more than a microphone used by the announcer at hockey games. To make matters worse, the whole place was stale, dank and dusty.

I was not a happy camper. After all, I was used to the best. It wasn't until I walked into the men's bathroom and caught a glimpse of myself in the mirror that I realized the truth. As I stood there sulking and feeling sorry for myself, the face staring back at me was that of a spoiled, petulant brat.

"Who are you to demand limos and fancy venues?" I asked my reflection. "These people are as honest, genuine and welcoming as anyone, and they've provided the best they have."

I snapped myself into shape, straightened my tie, combed my hair, added a big smile and went out there to give them my best.

Looking back, I don't think I've ever made a more inspired, genuine presentation. What I remember most is the standing ovation they gave me. I also remember the warmth they showed me with their smiles and handshakes. I flew home feeling exhilarated, having learned an important life lesson about letting my ego and expectations get in the way of doing my job. I also learned that while fancy jets and limousines are nice, they've got nothing on genuine hospitality.

I think the aforementioned Sir Edmund Hillary's perspective on fame is one to be admired and emulated. "I was just an enthusiastic mountaineer of modest abilities who was willing to work quite hard and had the necessary imagination and determination. I was just an average bloke; it was the media that transformed me into a heroic figure. And try as I did, there was no way to destroy my heroic image. But as I learned through the years, as long as you didn't believe all that rubbish about yourself, you wouldn't come to much harm."

> **"Flattery is alright, so long as you don't inhale."**
> —*ADLAI STEVENSON*

CHAPTER 69

BANISH A BAD MOOD

Happiness is not the absence of problems, it is the ability to deal with them.

Are you having one of those days – or weeks – when every little thing seems to annoy you? Are you wondering if that little black cloud will ever disperse, letting you enjoy the sunshine once again? Instead of putting up with feeling down, try these five simple steps to help identify and banish whatever's ailing you.

1. Stop and listen to what's on your mind. Be your own best friend and give yourself an

> "My therapist told me the way to achieve true inner peace is to finish what I start. So far I've finished two bags of M&Ms and a chocolate cake. I feel better already."
>
> —*DAVE BARRY*

empathetic ear. What exactly is it that's bothering you? What are you feeling? Disappointment? Resentment? Jealousy? Frustration? Admitting to yourself what you are really feeling is a good first step.

2. Give yourself a few minutes to ruminate on whatever it is that's bothering you. If you're feeling resentful or disappointed, just own it. We all have feelings we're not proud of or that aren't quite rational. Ignoring them doesn't make them go away; it just makes us feel worse.

3. Give yourself a pep talk. Here again, being your own best friend is the key. What would a good friend say to give you a morale boost? OK, now say it to yourself! Your subconscious doesn't care where the encouragement comes from, only that it gets what it needs to feel better.

4. Refocus on your goals. Remind yourself what is important to you and that you aren't going to let anyone or anything distract, deter or derail you from your priorities. Let your passion recharge your batteries.

5. Remember to laugh at yourself. You can take what you do seriously, just don't take *yourself* too seriously. Remember: in the end no one gets out alive, so you may as well enjoy every moment you can.

CHAPTER 70

I CAN'T AFFORD IT

I was on the same program with renowned speaker and author David Chilton recently. One of the best pieces of advice that David offers in *The Wealthy Barber Returns* is found in a chapter titled "Four Liberating Words." Here, a friend asks him for advice on controlling his spending, after divulging that his income can't keep pace with his lifestyle because of invites to dinner, to hockey games and trips to the golf course. Chilton's advice to him is simple, "Sometimes when people ask you to do something, you just have to say, 'I can't afford it.' "

The friend is surprised that's all the advice he has to offer but agrees to try it out. A month later, Chilton asks if he wants to go for dinner and he says, point blank, "I can't afford it." The friend then goes on to explain how liberating it was to start using those four words and what a relief it was not to feel pressured to do things he couldn't afford, based on his own priorities.

It takes courage and a strong sense of yourself to say "I can't afford it," but it also sends the important message that you have goals and priorities you're not willing to sacrifice for a little bit of immediate gratification. That's not always easy, but as Chilton points out, it's a good starting point as an acceptance of reality; he notes that, for most people, using these four words is generally followed by a deep sense of relief.

Chilton says that when we spend money, we're often attempting to buy status and secure our place in the world. So many of our purchases are made with the aim of making a statement, but the truth is that most of the people around us are too caught up in their own life to really pay attention, so essentially we're wasting both our time and our money trying to impress people who don't care and live up to some imaginary standard.

A better approach: spend some time making a list of your goals and priorities and then put together a budget that supports those goals. Not only will this give you an out when offers and opportunities come up that aren't on your list (allowing you to decisively say "no thanks"), it will also really help to set priorities and free up more money for the things that are truly important to you.

CHAPTER 71

THE CHARLES SCHULZ PHILOSOPHY

I t's funny how things get started on the Internet; somebody shares something and says it was written or spoken by someone famous and suddenly the claim takes on a life of its own and quickly spreads.

One such bit is a quiz that has been attributed to *Peanuts* comic strip creator Charles Schulz. Although the people who run the Charles M. Schulz museum insist the quiz was not created by Schulz, it does at least contain a genuine quote from the man himself. Originally featured in the *Peanuts* comic strip in 1980, it reads: "Don't worry about the world coming to an end today . . . It's already tomorrow in Australia."

I always loved the *Peanuts* gang and the gentle humour of Charlie Brown, Snoopy, Linus, Lucy and Sally, among many other delightful characters. The comic strip has been around since 1950 and has run in more than 2,000 newspapers around the world, in many different languages. There was even a big-screen *Peanuts* movie in 2015. I never had the opportunity to meet Charles Schulz, who died in 2000, and even if he didn't write the quiz that is so often attributed to him, I'm sure he would have approved of the lesson it teaches.

You don't have to actually answer the questions below, just think about how many you actually know the answer to:

1.   Name the five wealthiest people in the world.
2.   Name the last five Heisman trophy winners.
3.   Name the last five winners of the Miss America pageant.
4.   Name 10 people who have won the Nobel or Pulitzer Prize.
5.   Name the last half-dozen Academy Award winners for best actor and actress.

How did you do? The point is, none of us remembers the headlines of yesterday. These are no second-rate achievers, they are the best in their fields. But the applause dies, awards tarnish, achievements are forgotten. Here's another quiz. See how you do on this one:

1.   List a few teachers who aided your journey through school.
2.   Name three friends who have helped you through a difficult time.

3. Name five people who have taught you something worthwhile.

4. Think of a few people who have made you feel appreciated and special.

CHAPTER 72

SIMPLY GIVE

T he great Law of Cause and Effect dictates that you and I live in a world in which everything happens for a reason. Sometimes it may not seem that way, but I believe that it's true. There are no accidents.

For example, it's no accident that so many of the most successful people in the world, such as Bill Gates and Oprah Winfrey, have discovered a great sense of fulfillment from giving back to the communities that helped make them successful.

An infatuated follower once told Mother Teresa that he intended to follow her around the world to learn her philanthropic secrets firsthand. He bought a plane ticket and was about to embark with her on a trip to South America, another leg in her worldwide, lifelong mission of service. Mother Teresa was flattered, but said simply: "Sell your ticket. Give the money to the poor."

It was a simple, yet profound lesson.

We can line up to shake hands with kings, queens, prime ministers and movie stars and probably learn nothing. Those same kings, queens, prime ministers and movie stars would line up to meet Mother Teresa, who would simply say "give," then go off on her quiet way, leaving the rest of us standing in open-mouthed wonder to ponder her wisdom.

As Mother Teresa and other spiritual visionaries such as the Dalai Lama have been telling us all along, making the world a better place isn't complicated. All we need to do is find someone who could use our gifts and talents (a charity, advocacy group or even an individual) and offer them up, no strings attached.

CHAPTER 73

LET IT GO

It's important to keep our lives free of unnecessary things. Famed self-help author Og Mandino puts it beautifully in the following quote that speaks of our actions as well as the possessions we accumulate.

"Never again clutter your days and nights with so many menial and unimportant things that you have no time to accept a real challenge when it comes along. This applies to play as well as work. A day merely survived is no cause for celebration. You are not here to fritter away your precious hours when you have the ability to accomplish so much by making a slight change in your routine. No more busy work. No more hiding from success. Leave time, leave space to grow. Now. Now! Not tomorrow!"

My old friend Joe Segal once told me, "If you don't need something, rather than hold onto it, give it to someone who does." For many of us, that's easy to say but hard to do. It's amazing how attached we have become to all of "our stuff," as the late comedian George Carlin famously joked about. The scary part is that for many people it is really getting out of control.

Maclean's magazine did a story on North America's fastest-growing real estate segment, the storage business, which generates $22 billion per year in revenue. In fact, in the span of just one decade, the amount of land devoted to this kind of storage in the United States has more than doubled to an area larger than Manhattan and San Francisco combined.

Interestingly, the article notes that many of the people who rent these storage lockers have a greater volume of "stuff" in storage than they have in their own homes and they are paying money to keep it there because they don't have room for it anywhere else. Imagine how much easier and less complicated their lives would be if they just got rid of some of it.

So, here's the question you knew I was eventually going to ask: "What part of your life needs tidying up?" Is it your basement, your car, your desk at work, your computer hard drive, that drawer or closet where you put everything that doesn't have a place? Maybe it's all of these.

Clearing out the stuff in your life that you no longer need or use doesn't just get rid of old junk that's getting in your way; it also frees up your mind and creates room for you to move forward with important plans and goals. So instead of storing, make a decision on what can stay and what needs to go, and then take action.

When you've rid your life of unnecessary things, suddenly you'll have a much clearer view of the important ones and you'll feel infinitely more productive, with more room to think and breathe.

CHAPTER 74

APPRECIATE YOUR
OWN VALUE

As a professional speaker, I know the importance of getting an audience's attention to drive a point home and nothing gets people's attention like offering them free money. Here's what one well-known speaker did to make a point.

As he started his seminar with a group of about 200 people, the speaker held up a $100 bill in his hand and asked, "Who would like this $100?"

Not surprisingly, hands shot up all around the room. Then he said, "I am going to give this money to one of you, but first let me do this." He crumpled the $100 bill up in his hand. He then asked, "Who still wants it?"

Still the hands went up in the air.

"Well," he said, "what if I do this?" And he dropped the money and started to grind it into the floor with his shoe. "Now who wants it?"

Still, hands shot up.

"Isn't that interesting?" he asked the rapt audience. "No matter what I did to the money, you still wanted it because even though it was crunched up and dirty, you knew that did not decrease its value. It is still worth $100."

Many times in our lives, we are dropped, crumpled and ground into the dirt by the decisions we make and the circumstances that come our way. As a result, sometimes we start to feel as though we're worthless. But no matter what has happened or what will happen, remember that you will never lose your value.

CHAPTER 75

THE POWER OF THOUGHT

I've always believed our thinking plays an integral part in the success we seek. If you've read my weekly *Insight* e-newsletter over the years, you've heard me say a number of times, "You become what you think about most of the time." That was a quote that helped shape my thinking by the aforementioned Earl Nightingale, widely considered the dean of motivational speakers.

The book *The Five Secrets You Must Discover Before You Die* by Dr. John Izzo (who is a fine speaker and author), deals with our thoughts and the power of positive thinking.

You might want to keep this in mind as you go about your daily routine:

- Be careful of your thoughts, because your thoughts become your words.
- Be careful with your words,
  because your words become your action.
- Be careful of your actions,
  because your actions become your habits.
- Be careful of your habits,
  because your habits become your character
  and your character becomes your destiny.

CHAPTER 76

THE LAWS OF PHYSICS AND LIFE

"Everybody shares one universal problem. To succeed you have to persuade others to support your vision, dream or cause." —Peter Guber

There are some physical laws and some laws of life that, no matter what happens, do not change.

One of them is the law of gravity. I won't go into why gravity does what it does, because I don't know. What I do know if that if you trip, chances are you'll fall and if you jump from the top of a tall building, you won't fly like Superman. Instead you will begin to plummet at a rate of 32 feet per second and continue to fall ever faster until you hit the ground. At that point, other laws of physics come into play, causing horrible things to happen to your body. (Please don't test this, just trust me.) The law of gravity works the same for all of us, young or old, rich or poor, tall or short, male or female. When it comes to jumping off buildings we all travel at the same rate.

Another important principle to remember in life is what we give out is what we get back. Send out anger, you get it back. Disrespect others and disrespect will soon come your way. Smile and some will look the other way because they think you're crazy, but most will smile back and share in the sense of goodwill.

Zig Ziglar said you can get everything you want or need in life if you just help enough people get what they want and need. You keep giving, you keep getting. It's a simple but powerful law.

But, as I touched on earlier, helping others doesn't just include helping those who are in an obvious position to do something for you in return. How you treat the "little people" in your life says a lot about you. By "little people" I mean those who are unlikely to be in a position to cause you any significant trouble even if you're being a first-class jerk. This includes people such as cleaning staff, administrative assistants, greeters or call centre operators. It also includes anyone who works under you within the structure of your organization.

Leaders of character are concerned with everyone in their organization. As a result, they are attentive to all followers and show them respect. The legendary UCLA basketball coach John Wooden was someone who personified this aspect of good character. I have heard many people share their stories of the attention and respect he showed to everyone he came into contact with. Here's what John had to say about character: "Be more concerned with your character than your reputation, because your character is what you really are, while your reputation is merely what others think you are."

Other revered business leaders are also famous for treating people with respect. Southwest Airlines CEO Herb Kelleher was renowned for his frequent visits to flight crews, during which he called employees by name and stopped to chat with them. Google CEO Larry Page also strives to maintain an open culture with employees, and every week average "Googlers" have an opportunity to pose questions directly to Page and other executives about anything related to the company.

If you don't care about others, why should they care about you, your business, your goals or your customers? When you are the leader, the way you treat people sets the tone for everyone else. Over time, that behaviour (and attitude) will filter through to every aspect of your enterprise.

Only send out into the world that which you hope to receive in return.

CHAPTER 77

IT'S WHAT YOU LEARN AFTER YOU KNOW IT ALL THAT COUNTS

S peaking of John Wooden, it took me most of a weekend to read his autobiography. The book is long, but a very good, insightful read, detailing, among other things, how he led his teams to 10 national titles.

One of the key lessons I took away from it revolves around what you learn after you know it all. Following are some of the lessons everyone should pay attention to, whether they think they know it all or not.

Never stop learning.
Think of yourself as a traveller and always try to look at the world around you with fresh eyes. When we are at home and

busy in our day-to-day lives, we get stuck in our routines and find it easy to say "no" to ideas and experiences; however, when we travel, we're much more open and because we don't know what to expect, we end up seeing and doing things we never thought we would. Keep that sense of openness and try saying "yes" more often.

Don't be afraid to get in over your head.

Of all the uncomfortable experiences, getting in over your head is probably the one most worth pursuing. Sure, it's a little scary and there's always the chance of failure, but nothing stretches you more or makes you more creative than having no idea what you're doing.

If you want to move up in your career, you must do things that get you noticed. Take on the big challenges and projects that no one else wants. It may not always be fun, but you will almost always be better for the effort and others will see that you are motivated to learn and grow.

Learn to give and take critical feedback.

We all want to get better at what we do. In order for that to happen, we have to be open to feedback from others. Learning to hear criticism without tuning out or disregarding what is being said may be one of the most positive things you can do for your career. So instead of taking it personally, think of critical feedback as a cheat sheet. In giving you direct feedback, your boss, colleague, mentor or coach is giving you a shortcut for getting better at the things that will help you be successful.

Sometimes, even when you make a real effort, taking feedback well can be a struggle. Your first impulse may be to protect yourself and get defensive or stop listening. Be aware of that. Prepare yourself by taking a breath when you realize critical feedback is coming your way, then listen to the whole thing without interruption. Write down what you've heard if that helps you process it and ask questions to make sure you're interpreting the feedback correctly. Once you understand what you're doing, you can come up with a plan to do better.

On the flip side of taking critical feedback is giving it to someone else. Whether you're a manager or a friend, feedback is an opportunity to help someone get better, so don't skip over it even if it makes you uncomfortable. Good coaches understand the importance of providing direct feedback and doing so in a respectful way. It's important not to try to soften the blow or talk around what it is you need to say. That might make you feel better but it will only confuse the issue and frustrate the other person. If you're struggling to be direct, try framing the issue in one clear sentence followed by some details to back up what you're saying. For example, "Fred, the way you're handling your sales calls isn't working. Let's talk through why . . ."

Feedback is also more constructive and effective when it is accompanied by recent, specific examples. Telling someone they have a bad attitude isn't helpful – it's far better to point to a precise moment when that bad attitude showed up and then explain how moments like that add up and impact others. Ultimately, knowing how to improve is as important as knowing *what* to improve, so the person receiving the feedback should leave the conversation feeling empowered to change, not demoralized.

CHAPTER 78

FIND A MENTOR . . . OR TWO . . . OR THREE . . .

I f you have heard me speak before or read any of my
other books (including this one), you know I am very
keen on mentors. That's because I have been blessed
in my lifetime to receive support and encouragement from
three of the best mentors. My first mentor was Raymond J.
Addington, former president of Kelly Douglas. Ray taught me
the significance of character and follow-through. My second
mentor is Dr. Mel Cooper, owner of CFAX Radio in Victoria.
You might also remember him as the vice-president of Expo
86. I first met Mel when I worked at CKNW before I was
married. Mel taught me the importance of a good attitude. He
once told me, "Your attitude determines your altitude. How

high you go is almost entirely due to a positive attitude." My third mentor is Dr. Joseph Segal, the legendary businessman and philanthropist who taught me the importance of communication, sharing ideas and never giving up.

Nobody is really successful unless other people want them to be. Mentors are people who choose you as much as you choose them. Your responsibility as the recipient of their wisdom is to lead a life that models the qualities that they have nurtured in you.

Help others be successful.
As success coach Brian Tracy says, "Successful people are always looking for opportunities to help others. Unsuccessful people are always asking, 'What's in it for me?' " The truth is, our greatest successes in life often come through helping others to succeed, and without question, when you focus on helping others succeed your eventual payoff will always be far greater than your investment. This is something I also learned from Joe Segal, who said, "Alone, you are only as good as your reach; you must join hands with others." According to Joe, joining together with others whose skills complement our own and who we can depend on to have our back, not only gives us courage, it also allows us to play to our strengths, thereby accomplishing far more than we ever could on our own.

Pass on the knowledge you've acquired.

I'm sure you've probably had a few moments in your career when you've thought to yourself, "I wish someone would have told me about such and such." I know I have. A lot of times, the road to success can feel more like a rollercoaster, with all the ups and downs and stomach-churning loops it entails. But now that you have all of this knowledge and life experience under your belt, don't keep it to yourself, put it to work and pass it on.

Life's too short.

In 2005, Steve Jobs delivered a commencement address to the graduating class of Stanford University. Interestingly, Jobs himself was not a college graduate, although that never got in the way of his success. In his address, Jobs focused on the importance of finding a purpose. Here is part of what he had to say: "Your time is limited, so don't waste it living someone else's life. Don't be trapped by dogma – which is living with the results of other people's thinking. Don't let the noise of other people's opinions drown out your own inner voice. And most important, have the courage to follow your heart and intuition; they somehow already know what you truly want to become. Everything else is secondary."

When my daughters were young we made a point of introducing them to different foods, including vegetables. While we didn't believe in forcing them to eat foods they really didn't like, our philosophy was that they at least had to try what was on their plate.

So it was that we attempted to get Samantha to eat brussels sprouts at Sunday dinner. As usual, when dinner was ready, my wife Kay served up a small portion of vegetables to each child. Unfortunately for Samantha, when the brussels sprouts landed on her plate it was not love at first sight. As dinner progressed, she managed to eat around the offending vegetables and thinking herself finished, asked to be excused.

"No, you may not," Kay said firmly. "You haven't even tried the brussels sprouts."

"I don't want to try them," said Samantha. "I already know I don't like them."

Not one to give in, Kay held her ground. "When you've finished what's on your plate you may be excused."

After sitting at the table glaring at the two lonely sprouts for half an hour, Samantha decided to negotiate (a tactic I would highly recommend to any child in a similar situation).

"If I eat these two brussels sprouts," she propositioned, "do you promise I'll never have to try them again?"

"Absolutely," Kay agreed. "As long as you try them."

Looking as if a life sentence had been lifted, Samantha quickly ate them up and excused herself.

Years later, while I was writing a book, I mentioned to

Samantha that I was thinking of including this story in a chapter on priorities.

"Yeah, dad," she said. "That would make a good chapter. After all, life's too short to eat brussels sprouts."

CHAPTER 79

A THOUSAND GOODBYES

My father, Bernie Legge, emigrated to Canada in 1952. He settled in New Westminster. Being alone (my mother and I were still in England that first year), he lived in the YMCA on Royal Avenue at first. He knew no one, not a single soul.

After almost a year of doing odd jobs, including picking berries on a Fraser Valley farm and washing dishes in a restaurant on Kingsway in Vancouver, he was discouraged. Feeling like he had failed in his dream to make a new life for his family in Canada, he agreed to take a contract job for six months in Kitimat to earn money to sail back home to England.

The day before he was scheduled to travel to Kitimat,

dad heard about an inside sales position at Gilley Brothers, a well-respected and admired company in the Royal City/ New Westminster. The interview went so well, the company hired him on the spot and my dad ended up spending the remainder of his working life at Gilley Brothers – until he turned 65, which was the mandatory retirement age at the time.

He left Gilley Brothers as one of the most successful sales-people ever, with a reputation for being a man of integrity and character. I remember hearing him on the phone at our house almost every night, making plans for the next house that he would build in the city of Coquitlam, which was the up-and-coming neighbourhood at that time. Contractors, builders, designers – they all wanted to do business with my dad and with Gilley Brothers. They trusted him.

Once he had a job, dad began to get involved with community organizations – a lot of community organizations! All of them in New Westminster, his newfound home. They included the New Westminster Chamber of Commerce, the Vagabond Theatre, the Hyack Festival organization, Royal City Ballet Society, the Miss New Westminster Pageant and the Royal City Musical Society. Eventually, he became the president of both the Hyack Festival and the Chamber of Commerce.

Dad also taught contestants in the New Westminster Pageant how to walk, sit and speak onstage, in addition to lessons on character and deportment. Even today, women will come up to me and say, "I was one of Bernie's Girls," referring to his role as the coordinator of speech, deportment and etiquette, which shows just how much of an impact he had on their lives after just six weeks.

Here's an excerpt from a speech delivered at the Hyack Festival in 2015 by one of Bernie's Girls, Becci Dewinetz, Miss New Westminster 1981:

"During the years he dedicated his time to our Miss New Westminster program, over 100 young ladies had the privilege of working with such a gentleman. Bernie had such an incredible gift of making everyone around him feel very special and important. When you spoke, he was genuinely interested in what you had to say, which is wonderful for a young girl who is building her confidence."

As a result of all of his contributions, dad received many honours, including citizen of the year. There is also a Bernie Legge Cultural Award presented each year and the New Westminster pageant has both an award and a scholarship in his name. In addition, the Vagabond Playhouse was renamed "The Bernie Legge Theatre." Not because he was a great actor, but because of what he stood for.

My dad died at the Royal Columbian Hospital in 1997. Almost 1,000 people came to his funeral.

From not knowing a single person in Canada to having 1,000 people come to say goodbye – that's something. In my opinion, it was due not just to his charm, but to his integrity, his outstanding decency as a human being and to his good character; all of which speaks volumes about the kind of man he was.

Three of the most important life lessons I learned from my father:

1. Never give up on your dreams; it might take a lot of hard work, but it's worth it. He stuck it out in Canada and ended up building a wonderful life for himself in his new homeland.

2. People remember the way you treat them and they notice what kind of person you are. If you think no one is watching and paying attention to how you conduct yourself, you're wrong. Every person you come in contact with deserves to be treated with compassion and understanding.

3. Spend your days pursuing the things you want said at your funeral.

CONCLUSION

Abraham Lincoln once said, "You cannot escape the responsibility of tomorrow by evading today."

My friend Nido Qubein, president of High Point University in North Carolina and a much in-demand speaker, said, "Your past does not determine your future."

Seize today and begin putting into practice your desired dreams and objectives. Realizing success doesn't suddenly occur in one day, or one week or over one year. Then again, neither does failure.

It takes a decision to improve yourself day-by-day. Read, study, learn, seek mentors who will encourage you and hold you accountable, and go boldly into your business community and contribute to its life; by doing so you will also grow your own life.

Napoleon Hill said, "The No. 1 disease of business leaders in North America is procrastination." We put off today what can easily be put off again tomorrow, next week and next year, and if we are not careful a whole decade goes by without us even realizing.

I wish I had written this line – I can't seem to find its author: "You were born with the seeds of greatness, but to manifest those seeds and grow them, you must take action today so you can be all that God wants you to be."

Knock and ask and the door will open.

If you've ever studied Hebrew, here's what it says about success: "It is the ability to make wise decisions." That's it! Wise decisions.

Sow nothing – reap nothing; the decision is yours.

Good luck and God bless.

ABOUT THE AUTHOR

PETER LEGGE, O.B.C. • LL.D. (Hon) • D.Tech. • CSP • CPAE • HoF

Peter Legge is an inspiration to anyone who meets him. He lives his life's dream as an internationally acclaimed professional speaker, bestselling author and as chairman and CEO of the largest, independently owned magazine publishing company in Western Canada — Canada Wide Media Limited. Peter is a community leader who tirelessly devotes his time to many worthwhile organizations and was recently named one of the 2012 top-25 immigrant entrepreneurs in Canada.

His presentations are based on his everyday experiences as a community leader, husband, father and CEO. Peter has published 19 previous books, his most recent being *My Favourite Quotations*. His books have motivated thousands of people towards positive change.

Toastmasters International has voted Peter "Golden Gavel Award Winner" and "Top Speaker in North America," and both the National Speakers Association and the Canadian Association of Professional Speakers have inducted him into the Speakers Hall of Fame.

Peter is also a member of the prestigious Speakers Roundtable, an invitation-only society comprising 20 of North America's top professional speakers. He is the recipient of three honorary doctorate degrees, and in 2006, the Peter

Legge Philanthropist of the Year Award was introduced by the Canadian Association of Professional Speakers. Peter was the first recipient of this award.

In June 2008, the province's highest honour, the Order of British Columbia, was presented to Peter for his lifelong commitment to serving the community.

In the summer of 2012, Peter was honoured by Douglas College with the establishment of the Peter Legge International Institute of Sales Excellence. Later that same year, he was one of a number of recipients presented with the Queen's Diamond Jubilee Medal in honour of his significant achievements and contributions to British Columbia.

You can contact Peter Legge at:

Peter Legge Management Company Ltd.
#230 - 4321 Still Creek Drive
Burnaby, BC V5C 6S7 Canada

Telephone: 604.299.7311
Email: plegge@canadawide.com
Website: www.peterlegge.com

To order Peter's books, CDs and other products,
please visit **www.peterlegge.com**
or email **Heather Vince** at *hvince@canadawide.com*

If you would like to set up a speaking engagement with
Peter Legge please contact his assistant
Heather Vince at **604.473.0332**

Linkedin.com/in/peterblegge   @_peterlegge

To subscribe to Peter's complimentary business
e-newsletter "Insight," email *hvince@canadawide.com*